Praise for *The Truth About Negotiations*

"All too often, we think of single-issue negotiations that by their nature become zero sum. This book expands our thinking and puts as much effort into creating value and expanding the pie as we dedicate to getting our fair share of value or dividing the pie. A great read for anyone involved in negotiating."

Anthony Santiago, Vice President,
Global Sourcing & Supplier Management,
Bristol-Myers Squibb

"The 53 Truths provide incredible insight into the art and science of negotiating. This is a must read for sales professionals but is equally beneficial to all those who wish to be better negotiators."

Chris Weber, Vice President,
West Region Enterprise,
Microsoft Corporation

"A superbly presented summary of practical tools and techniques for negotiating in all types of situations, and creating win-win solutions that result in enduring business relationships. Provides substantiated evidence of what works successfully—and pitfalls to avoid—in the game of negotiation."

Russell D'Souza, International Credit Manager,
Hallmark Cards, Inc.

THE TRUTH ABOUT

NEGOTIATIONS

Leigh Thompson

FT Press offers excellent discounts on this
book when ordered in quantity for bulk purchases
or special sales. For more information, please
contact U.S. Corporate and Government Sales,
1-800-382-3419, corpsales@pearsontechgroup.
com. For sales outside the U.S., please contact
International Sales at international@pearsoned.com.

Company and product names mentioned herein are
the trademarks or registered trademarks of their
respective owners.

Printed in the United States of America

Fifteenth Printing   October 2011

ISBN-10: 0-13-600736-8
ISBN-13: 978-0-13-600736-4

Pearson Education LTD.
Pearson Education Australia PTY, Limited.
Pearson Education Singapore, Pte. Ltd.
Pearson Education North Asia, Ltd.
Pearson Education Canada, Ltd.
Pearson Educatión de Mexico, S.A. de C.V.
Pearson Education—Japan
Pearson Education Malaysia, Pte. Ltd.

Vice President, Publisher
Tim Moore

**Associate Editor-in-Chief
and Director of Marketing**
Amy Neidlinger

Acquisitions Editor
Jennifer Simon

Editorial Assistant
Pamela Boland

Development Editor
Russ Hall

Digital Marketing Manager
Julie Phifer

Publicist
Amy Fandrei

Marketing Coordinator
Megan Colvin

Cover and Interior Designs
Stuart Jackman,
Dorling Kindersley

Managing Editor
Gina Kanouse

Senior Project Editor
Lori Lyons

Copy Editor
Karen Gill

Proofreader
San Dee Phillips

Design Manager
Sandra Schroeder

Compositor
Gloria Schurick

Proofreader
San Dee Phillips

Manufacturing Buyer
Dan Uhrig

Library of Congress Cataloging-in-Publication Data

Thompson, Leigh L.
  The truth about negotiations / Leigh L. Thompson.
    p. cm.
  ISBN 0-13-600736-8 (pbk. : alk. paper) 1. Negotiation. 2. Interpersonal
communication. I. Title.
  BF637.N4T455 2008
  302.3--dc22

                                              2007025667

Contents

You spend more time negotiating than you do driving to work each day. Most of us take our driving seriously: We've studied, practiced, and taken a driving test. We have a license, insurance, a car, and a fancy navigation system; we know the rules of the road, and we hope that people who disobey those rules will get pulled over and ticketed. These investments mean that we don't sit up at night worrying about how we are going to drive ourselves to work. We have the equipment, we know what we are doing, and we get there. We feel ready, prepared.

Going to negotiation every day should be the same way. Yet, if you are like most people, you spend countless hours fretting about upcoming negotiations. "What should I say?" "Should I open first or no?" "What do I do if they don't accept my offer?" and so on.

This book is about how to make sure you are prepared and ready to negotiate on the roughest of terrain, with the most daunting road conditions.

The need to negotiate can happen at any time—sometimes once a day, and sometimes more than once a day. Any time you cannot reach your goals without the cooperation of someone else, you are propelled headlong into negotiation. You may not be engaged in a hostage negotiation, or striking a deal for millions of dollars worth of a product or service for a company, but the importance of arriving at a point where you and the other party both feel you win is as vital to your peace, sanity, and productiveness. For example, if your goal is to eat dinner in peace and your young child is demanding that you fix a toy or play a game, you must negotiate.

If your goal is to sell your house and upgrade to a nicer house with a heftier mortgage, you must negotiate with your penny-pinching spouse, who may not be up for the move. You sometimes are thrown into negotiations when you least expect it—such as when somebody has the nerve to claim what you thought was yours. Imagine that a coworker announces he or she wants to "reconsider" the project responsibilities that you thought you both already agreed to. Or your neighbor claims it is your job to repair a fence that fell down after a freak thunderstorm.

The simple question I ask in this book is: "*Are you ready to negotiate at the drop of a hat?*" If your answer is anything but "Yes, certainly," then please read on. One false move in negotiations of major importance, such as salary negotiations, house buying, and car buying can have a dramatic negative consequence on your economic welfare for years to come. Given that your quality of life is affected by your ability to bring home the bacon as well as eat it in quiet dignity, knowing how to negotiate in the corporate world and in the kitchen is essential for peace of mind and retirement.

This book does three things: First, it provides a game plan that works in any negotiation situation. I dispel the faulty belief that negotiations in boardrooms or real estate deals are fundamentally different from salary negotiations, school and community negotiation...and, yes, negotiations with spouses and kids. Chances are, if you are great at making real estate deals, then you also will be great at negotiating with a caterer for your local charity's fund-raiser.

Second, this book focuses on the two key tasks of any negotiation: how to create win-win deals by leveraging information carefully collected from the other party, and how to effectively lay claim to part of the win-win goldmine.

Finally, this book talks about how to handle less-than-perfect situations, such as when you make a threat (that you did not really mean), how to establish trust with someone you don't trust, how to walk away at the right time, and negotiating with people you don't really like, and at the other end of the spectrum, who you love very much.

Negotiation may sound daunting, but if you are informed, practiced, and prepared, even you can do it. And that's the truth.

TRUTH

1

If you have only one hour to prepare...

Negotiation does not just occur in used car lots, boardrooms, or lawyers' offices. You negotiate every day: with your spouse to split up household tasks, with your colleagues regarding who will take a client's call, with your young kids to determine the best time for bed. Any time meeting your goals requires the cooperation of others, you must negotiate.

Sometimes you have significant time to prepare for a negotiation. But other times you get blindsided: You get a call from an old friend with a "hot" business opportunity. Or you receive a disturbing email from a colleague claiming resources you believe to be yours. Or your nanny or assistant threatens to leave unless you give her a raise and a three-week vacation. In all these situations, you may feel there's no time to prepare for negotiation.

But even if you've got only an hour—or just moments—to prepare, there are several crucial steps you have to take.

1. Identify your key goals.
2. Brainstorm your options.
3. Plan your opening move.

Get in touch with your goals

Negotiators are often quick to stake out a position. A position is a demand, such as, "I want a bonus check!" The danger in stating a position is that it can lead the other party to stake out a position, such as, "No way; I'm not paying you a bonus!"

Conversely, negotiators who move past positions to focus on their interests usually achieve their goals. A real goal reflects a negotiator's interests and answers the "why" question. Take the case of two colleagues negotiating who gets the more spacious office in a suite. It would be easy for both colleagues to say, "I want the bigger office." That is a demand. If the colleagues articulate why they desire the bigger office, they are getting closer to stating their goals. For example, one colleague might want the larger office because it would allow her to have team meetings that are currently impossible to schedule in

> Any time meeting your goals requires the cooperation of others, you must negotiate.

a conference room, and she is under pressure to deliver on a deadline. The other colleague might want the office to impress important clients.

People's demands may be incompatible, but their goals might be compatible or at least complementary. For example, if the two colleagues articulate their goals, they might create an arrangement in which they share the big office, reserving it for meetings with clients.

People's demands may be incompatible, but their goals might be compatible or at least complementary.

Brainstorm your options

Negotiations do not always end in mutual settlement. A colleague may pull rank to acquire the big office; the nanny may quit; the company may not take your offer. So you need to face the thorny question of what you would do in the absence of agreement. In short, what are your alternative courses of action? Most people have tunnel vision when it comes to their alternative courses of action in a negotiation. They are so focused on their demands that they can't see all the different paths through the forest. Identify your options using the four fundamental rules of brainstorming.[1]

- Suspend your initial judgment and just list all options that come to mind, even outlandish ones.

- Strive for quantity—often, a good idea emerges from several silly-sounding ones.

- Reserve judgment and evaluation until later.

- Mix, match, and combine different options.

Plan your opening move

Your opening offer should clearly articulate your goal and suggest how to reach it. ("I would like the corner office because my client load is highest in the office, and my team is unable to fit in the current space.") You don't need to blurt out your opening offer the moment you meet with the other party. But, at some point, after you exchange pleasantries or perhaps even after the other party places something on the table, it will be your turn to anchor the negotiation.

Your opening offer should represent the ideal situation for you. State it clearly, but do not position your offer as a demand. One direct but nondemanding way of doing this is, "In the spirit of getting the discussion started, I've mapped out a set of terms that works for me...." Or "I want to respect your time, so I have prepared a proposal that I would like to get your reaction to...."

Be firm on your interests but flexible on how to achieve them. Don't make take-it-or-leave-it demands. If you are feeling demanding or indignant before the negotiation, rehearse an opening that you might present to someone you care about (such as your spouse or friend)—even if you don't particularly care about the other party. The danger of making insulting, take-it-or-leave-it offers is that most people will opt to leave it.

TRUTH

2

Negotiation:
A natural gift?

I have never met a natural-born negotiator. The best negotiators I've met have been self-made, not manufactured by their parents. People can adapt and improve with conscious effort, and, in fact, that is the only path to becoming a good negotiator.

Nevertheless, a great number of people believe successful negotiation is all in the DNA, and that negotiation, like leadership, is something you're born with.

You don't have to travel far to see that the right kind of experience can dramatically improve your negotiation outcomes. The "magic bullet," when it comes to experiences that enhance negotiation skills, is the I-C-E rule.

- Give *immediate* feedback (preferably within one hour).
- Make the feedback *clear* to the point of indisputability.
- Give the negotiator the tools to be more *effective*.

Negotiation is something you can practice and improve upon. If, immediately after a simulation (within 20 minutes), someone could score you, interpret your score as clearly as possible, and give you a toolbox to ensure you didn't repeat mistakes, you would, with repetition, improve your negotiation skills. People's scores usually improve dramatically, by over 20 percent on average.

As you read this book, I suggest you follow the advice given to the person who asked how to get to Carnegie Hall. "Practice." Test the skills of each Truth, and, if possible, get prompt, clear feedback, and you will find yourself becoming more effective. Try negotiating on a personal level and test yourself. The more time and effort you put into trying out the various points and techniques shared, the more prepared you will be.

Your ability to do well in life's most important negotiations isn't determined by your basic personality or genetic structure. It's most strongly determined by a simple factor: your level of motivation to improve yourself.

> The best negotiators I've met have been self-made, not manufactured by their parents.

TRUTH

3

Rehearsal might get you to Carnegie, but it won't help you negotiate

Most people look for a magic bullet when it comes to negotiation, and well, there is one. Are you ready? Okay, here it is. *Prepare*. After years of offering this advice, sending people off, and expecting magic to occur that never did, I finally realized the problem: Rehearsing does not equal preparation.

There are two styles of preparation, and only one of them works. Let's call the two styles *Pattern X* and *Pattern Y*.

Pattern X Preparation

These activities seem to be useful but aren't.

- Rehearsing your demands
- Pumping yourself up
- Making a personal pledge to yourself or your partner to act tough
- Figuring out how to throw off the other negotiators or make them feel uncomfortable, which includes rearranging furniture (putting their chairs in odd positions)
- Preparing backhanded compliments and outright insults
- Rehearsing phrases that include, "This is my final offer"; "My bottom line"; "This is a deal-breaker"; "Nonnegotiable"; and "Then we don't have a deal"
- Framing your opening offer as a demand

Pattern Y Preparation

These activities are extraordinarily useful, but negotiators often don't engage in them.

- Listing all issues under consideration (e.g., payment, terms and conditions, indemnities, volume, distribution)
- Arranging those issues in order of importance or priority to you (either by using a simple rank-order or allocating 100 points among the issues to reflect what percentage of overall importance each represents)
- For each issue, brainstorming all the alternatives (for example, payment terms might range from 0 percent down to paid-in-full)
- Brainstorming issues the other party might bring up

- Identifying your most desirable set of terms for each of the issues
- Identifying and prioritizing your alternative courses of action to negotiating with this person (for example, liquidating your product)
- Identifying the other party's potential alternative courses of action
- Preparing an opening offer as a way of starting discussions

If negotiators did even a subset of these activities to prepare for a negotiation, they would fare dramatically better than if they didn't. In other words, Pattern Y negotiators have measurably better outcomes than do Pattern X negotiators. Pattern X is more likely to strike out; Pattern Y gets you to yes.

The question, then, is how to get people to follow Pattern Y when most of them are used to Pattern X? Clearly, relying on natural instinct won't work. So let me suggest you use a strategy I call *guided preparation*. If unguided preparation is allowing negotiators to do whatever they want, guided

> **Pattern Y negotiators have measurably better outcomes than do Pattern X negotiators.**

preparation is giving them a step-by-step method to follow. Jeanne Brett at the Kellogg School devised an easy-to-follow model that you can use. It works like this.

1. List all the issues to be negotiated in the first column. (Be ready to add issues the other party brings up.)

2. For each of the issues listed, in the second column, indicate its relative importance to you (use either a rank order or allocate 100 points among the issues), your most desired terms, and your underlying interests.

3. For all issues, in the third column make your best guess about the counterparty's interests, rankings, and most desired terms.

If you have accomplished these three things, you can get some sleep, knowing you have prepared effectively.

TRUTH

4

The power of making the first offer

Conventional negotiation wisdom strictly cautions negotiators against opening first—to avoid tipping their hands. If everyone does this, you are liable to end up in a comical cat-and-mouse game in which both parties develop elaborate methods to avoid answering any questions as long as possible and eventually walk away without a deal.

I don't know the origin of this bad advice, but I'd like to banish it right now. I researched the scientific literature and explored numerous studies that have investigated negotiators' offer patterns and outcomes. In *none* of those investigations did it harm negotiators to open first. In fact, it appears to *always* benefit negotiators to open first. One caveat: *In the rare and undesirable situation in which the other party knows more about you than you know about him, it is a disadvantage to open first.*

Why does it work to open first?

Your opening offer acts as a powerful psychological anchor in a negotiation. It carries a lot of weight. Your opening represents the most you can (usually) hope to get. Don't underestimate how important opening offers are. Indeed, negotiators' first offers can generally predict the outcome of a negotiation. Adam Galinsky and Tomas Mussweiler found that first offers correlate as much as 85 percent of the time with outcomes.[2]

Many negotiators live in fear of the *winner's* curse, believing that the counterparty will gleefully and immediately accept their first offer. Don't come to the silly conclusion that you can make outrageous offers and expect to do well. Unfortunately, offers wildly outside the *zone of possible agreement* (ZOPA) lose their anchoring power and lead to a *chilling* effect, where a negotiator grows cold on a deal because he feels that the other party is not bargaining in good faith, or even the *boomerang effect*, which occurs when a ridiculous offer invites an equally ridiculous counteroffer, often as a matter of spite. For these reasons, your ideal offer should be close to the other party's barely-acceptable terms.

> Many negotiators live in fear of the *winner's curse*, believing that the counterparty will gleefully and immediately accept their first offer.

No one is going to accept your first offer, so making a concession is inevitable.

Strategically speaking, your aspiration point should be *slightly worse* (for the other party) than your guess about the other party's *best alternative to negotiated agreement* (BATNA). The logic: No one is going to accept your first offer, so making a concession is inevitable. If you open with an offer that matches the other party's barely acceptable terms, you'll never end up there. It's best, then, to open with a figure slightly worse than the *counterparty's barely acceptable terms.* If your opening offer is dramatically worse, you create a chilling effect. If it is just a tiny bit worse, you are in the domain of the counterparty's *acceptability range.* Offers in this range are, by definition, not insulting.

5

What if you don't make the first offer?

Once you know that scientific evidence supports the negotiator who makes the first offer, you may go so far as to cover your ears when you realize that the other party is about to present you with an opening offer.

But, it's not wise to tune the other party out if she is ready to make you an offer. A better strategy is simply to remind yourself of your own first offer before the other party delivers hers. Preparing your opening offer is your best defense. Under typical conditions, however, most people haven't prepared their opening and are swept out to sea when the other party opens first.

Here are some handy points to think about in advance.

- If you haven't prepared an opening offer, you shouldn't be at the bargaining table. Remember, your opening offer is a behavioral manifestation of your aspiration point. So it's imperative to prepare your opening offer.

- If you state your opening offer like a demand, you should fear either the chilling or the boomerang effect (discussed in Truth 4, "The power of making the first offer.") However, you *can* make your offer in a nondemanding way. Here's how I do it in my personal negotiations:

In the spirit of recognizing how important your time is, I have prepared a set of terms that would be acceptable to me. I understand, however, that you will most likely have some different ideas. So I offer this set of terms (which I have written on the flip chart over here) as a starting point for what I hope is a more broad-ranging discussion. And, in that spirit, I am eager to hear your ideas.

Suppose that the other party has indeed beaten you to the punch and has made one heck of an opening offer. In that case, I would say,

Thanks for sharing your ideas with me. I've also spent some time preparing a set of terms that would work for me. I will

If you haven't prepared an opening offer, you shouldn't be at the bargaining table.

warn you right now that my terms are dramatically different from the ones you've sketched. But, in the spirit of recognizing the value of your time and beginning our discussion, I'd like to share them with you. I am ready to fully discuss all terms.

- Okay, you got flustered. Everyone does occasionally. So, here's an idea: Always, I mean always, write down your opening offer. If you find yourself tongue tied, you can always pull out your notebook or turn your laptop around to share your ideas. Anchors work dramatically better when you write them down. So write down your opening offer on a flip chart or blackboard. That way, you can continue to refer to it during the discussion.

Always write down your opening offer.

TRUTH

6

Don't be a tough or a nice negotiator

Most people are under the impression that to succeed in negotiation, they've got to be tough or competitive. This makes many people uncomfortable because they want to succeed in negotiation but don't like acting tough. So, many opt to be cooperative, because they want the other party to like and trust them, and frankly it's just more comfortable. The downside: They often perform less well economically.

Some people act cooperative during simulated negotiations because it's more natural for them but then feel like "chumps" when their outcomes are poor. Other people have the opposite problem. They cannot see any wisdom in being cooperative, so they act very competitively during the negotiations and then wonder why no one likes them.

The enduring questions for negotiators then are, "Should I be tough and competitive or nice and cooperative? Do I want to succeed or do I want to build relationships?"

I firmly believe that tough versus nice is a *false choice*. You don't have to choose between them. To be a skilled negotiator, you do need to be fluent in the languages of both cooperation and competition. Let's examine "creating value" and "claiming value" in more detail.[3]

- **Creating value**—Creating value refers to "win-win" negotiation. It is the process of developing deals that represent mutual gains for all parties involved. To create value, we need to cooperate with the other parties and genuinely work with their interests in mind.

> To be a skilled negotiator, you do need to be fluent in the languages of both cooperation and competition.

Management guru Mary Parker Follett tells the story of two sisters quarreling over a single orange. Both sisters are strong, tough, and ultra-competitive, to the point that the only agreement they can reach is to split the orange in half. One sister squeezes the juice from her half to make fresh orange juice and discards the peel. The other sister grates her half of the peel for an orange scone recipe and throws out the juice. In the heat of the argument, the sisters overlooked a simple win-win solution: One sister gets the whole peel, the other all the juice. By the time they realize their error, the fruit's remains are gone. By acting purely competitively, the "Orange Sisters," who you will return to in later Truths, turned an easy win-win into a lose-lose. According to negotiation gurus Roger Fisher and Bill Ury, who wrote the book *Getting to Yes*, the two sisters communicated only their positions, not their interests.

■ **Claiming value**—No one wants to get no part of the orange or just a sliver. It's necessary to make claims in a negotiation. But making claims is different from making demands.

Sometimes people get so carried away creating value that they forget about their own bottom lines. Claiming value, then, refers to how negotiators garner resources for themselves and their companies.

Most people falsely believe that creating value (cooperating) and claiming value (competing) are opposite ends of the same continuum:

COMPETITIVE ———— COOPERATIVE

I disagree. It's simultaneously possible to be competitive *and* cooperative. The best state of affairs is to have a negotiator who is cooperative in working with the other party to understand and explore his issues and interests and competitive enough to claim valuable resources for himself.

It's simultaneously possible to competitive *and* cooperative.

TRUTH

7

Four sand traps in the golf game of negotiation

My dad has been a golfer for as long as I can remember. He had a golf analogy for almost every aspect of life.

The first time he took me golfing, I hit the ball straight into the first hole's sand trap. *"Is that good, Dad?" "No, it's not. It's hard to get out of there. You need to stay OUT of the sand traps in the first place."*

When I started seeing patterns in the underperformance of otherwise smart people at the negotiation table, it occurred to me to think of these problems as sand traps. Every negotiation table is like a golf course: We may not have played that exact course before, but all courses have sand traps, and it helps to know where they are. If we know where the problem spots are, we're in a better position to reach our goals. If we hit our ball into a marsh on the first hole, we may never recover.

This Truth outlines four sand traps. I've been in every one of them, and I'd sure like to see you avoid them.

Sand trap #1: Leaving money on the table

This is the case of a *lose-lose* negotiation. Lose-lose negotiation, not surprisingly, is the opposite of win-win. On average, people settle for terms worse for both parties in one out of every five negotiations![4] The problem is that they are unaware of the fact that win-win possibilities existed.

Sand trap #2: Settling for too little

This is also known as the *winner's curse*. Consider Ron, for example, who was in Kuwait during the Gulf War. During his time of service, Ron was engaged, and he wanted to buy his fiancée a gold necklace before he returned to the States. He spotted the perfect necklace in a Kuwait jewelry store. It was priced at about $600 U.S. dollars. Ron offered the merchant $300. "Sold!" the merchant said immediately, beaming. Ron was proud of his ability to get such a great deal. But the merchant was giddily happy and even offered Ron a free matching set of earrings. Ron's pride turned into regret. He had fallen prey to the winner's curse, which occurs when a negotiator's first proposal is immediately accepted by the other party, signaling that the offer was too generous.

When Ron realized he had fallen prey to the winner's curse, he couldn't easily retract his offer in good faith. The merchant had already packed the necklace and earrings in a charming gift box and embraced Ron, wishing him, "A wonderful married life!"

Sand trap #3: Walking away from the table

This is the "hubris" problem. Negotiators who are so prideful that they walk away from the table dramatically even when they have no other attractive options are essentially bluffing. They lack the good sense to swallow their pride and return to the table.

I have known several negotiators guilty of hubris. They often dig their own graves because once they have made a take-it-or-leave-it offer, they can't tolerate the thought of losing face by returning to the table. You may argue that it's important to display toughness and resolve to the other side. However, earning a reputation for being tough doesn't serve you well at the negotiation table. Indeed, a reputation as a tough negotiator leads to a number of highly undesirable outcomes—for example, counterparties will treat you with greater suspicion and act much tougher than they normally would. In a recent investigation of how bargaining reputation affects how others treat you, Cathy Tinsley of Cornell University found that "tough guys finish last," meaning that people negotiate more aggressively with those who have a reputation for toughness.[5]

Sand trap #4: Settling for terms that are worse than your current situation

I call this the "agreement bias." I use it to refer to the negotiator who is so desperate to make a deal that she literally forgets she has a better alternative and accepts the offer in the heat of the moment.

For example, if I currently have an offer of $300,000 for my home and your best offer to me is $295,000, it wouldn't be in my interest to make a deal with you, all other things being equal.

Nevertheless, negotiators often get swept away by a negotiation's momentum. Indeed, once we sit down at the table and invest in a relationship, we often feel bad walking away from it. Simply put, negotiators often rationalize accepting inferior terms.

Write your walk-away point on a piece of paper so you can refer to it before you accept a proposal.

To prevent this, write your walk-away point on a piece of paper so you can refer to it before you accept a proposal. Obviously, the writing should be encrypted so that the note wouldn't mean much more than a grocery shopping list if seen by the other party!

TRUTH

8

Your industry is unique (and other myths)

Contrary to popular thought, the basic structure of negotiation does not differ that much across different industries.

Myth #1: Your industry is unique

No matter what the industry, negotiators have specific issues that are important to them. For example, a home buyer might focus on price, closing date, and financing terms. A publisher might focus on royalty rate, permissions, copyright retention, and number of free author copies. The key thing for both of these negotiators is not the nuances of how closing dates and royalty rates work, but rather the fact that they both care about certain issues and may or may not be willing to make concessions in regard to them. Similarly, both the home buyer and publisher might have a "bottom line" and might be inclined to make threats. The parallels between negotiations in different industries far outnumber any differences.

Here's an analogy. Suppose your child said, "I really want to learn how to play card games, and I need to know 'card math.' Can you teach me?" Later that evening, your child says, "Can you please teach me basketball math to figure out players' stats?" Then at bedtime, "I have to figure out how to do candy math so when I buy candy I can count the change."

You'd probably say, "I have good news: There's no difference between card math, basketball math, and candy math. For that matter, there's no difference between grocery store math, checkbook math, and dessert math. Math is math. There are certain key rules and operators you can use whether you're playing poker, analyzing basketball stats, or buying lollipops. Once you know the rules, you can use them anywhere."

Negotiation is negotiation. Scientific principles apply to all of life's negotiations, from the most intimate to the most economic. In other words, you can use the same principles to negotiate with a loan officer that you can with a colleague or spouse.

> You can use the same principles to negotiate with a loan officer that you can with a colleague or spouse.

The fact that all negotiations (whether with nannies or Wall Street financiers) have predictable parallels is good news. Why? It means there's a science to negotiation, and once we crack the code, we can use our skills any time with anyone.

Also, you may start out in consulting, change to banking, and then end up in the government. Because of the parallels among negotiation types, you won't have to reinvent yourself each time—at least as a negotiator.

There are three more myths I want to clear up so that we're on the same page.

Myth #2: Business people care only about money

This is false. Business people seek to maximize their utility. So do professors, students, home buyers, parents, children, spouses, and professional wrestlers. Your utility is not your money. Your

> There's a science to negotiation, and once we crack the code, we can use our skills any time with anyone.

utility represents your overall satisfaction with a particular situation. When I negotiate with my child or someone else I care about, I want him to be happy, too. So his happiness is part of my utility, and in my negotiations with him, I am seeking to maximize my utility, which includes my welfare and his. Excellent salespeople know that customers are valuable, so part of their own utility is pleasing the customer.

Myth #3: Always maintain a poker face: Never reveal anything

This is false, too. We'll talk a lot more about this later. But for now, just think about how the Orange Sisters mentioned earlier in this section kept poker faces and never signaled their interests. And look what happened to them!

Myth #4: Never make the first offer

Again, this one's false. There isn't a single published scientific investigation that supports this advice in any way. I challenge you to find any scientific evidence that does. Yet many studies support the wisdom of making the first offer.

TRUTH

9

Identify your BATNA

A few months ago, my husband and I made a grave mistake in mindlessly allowing both of our sons (ages 10 and 11) to sign up for traveling basketball teams. At the time, I did not appreciate the literal meaning of the word "travel," but I found out quickly that for 10 weekends in a row, the entire family would be on the road and sitting in smelly gyms across the greater Midwest! Moreover, because these youth games start at the ungodly hour of 8 a.m., it became necessary to spend the night in a hotel the night before. Thus, our hotel bills started to mount perilously high.

On one occasion, the entire team had to travel to Wisconsin for two nights. Once I realized that all the families on the team were in the same position as we were, I recognized that I was in a potentially powerful negotiation position to negotiate blocks of rooms with hotels.

So, I started my research. I made an Excel list of all the hotels within a 10-mile radius of the gym. At the top of my list was a Holiday Inn that had a kids' water park. (None of the other nearby hotels did, so this was clearly my first choice.) I called the events manager and asked about getting a good rate for this block of rooms. Normally, the room rates were well above $200 a night.

When I found the Holiday Inn with the water park, I already had a fallback option, but not an attractive one. The Comfort Inn was not as nice as the Holiday Inn, but it was cheap. Yet, it had no "kid appeal" (which potentially meant that parents would be forced to do all the entertaining). The Comfort Inn was my *best alternative to negotiating an agreement* with the Holiday Inn.[6] The Comfort Inn, therefore, was my BATNA! Having a BATNA helped me to leverage my power in the negotiation with the Holiday Inn, where we got a *very* good rate.

*   *   *

Some time ago, a friend came to me to seek advice. Our conversation went something like this:

Friend: "I'm glad Company X made me an offer, but the offer isn't that great. I want a higher salary, better benefits, a signing bonus, and moving expenses. My friends are all getting those."

Me: "What will you do if they don't improve the offer?"

Friend: "What do you mean?"

Me: "How many other job offers do you have?"

Friend: "Just this one. But it's a good company!"

Me: "Have you ever heard of a BATNA? Your key source of power in a negotiation is your ability to walk away, which depends on your BATNA. It's the power of alternatives."

Friend: "I don't have a BATNA!"

Me: "Calm down. You do have a BATNA. You always have a BATNA. What you're saying is that you don't *like* your BATNA. It's unattractive to you. But you have one."

What I mean by "You always have a BATNA" is that you will always do something if you fail to reach an agreement with the other party, even if it means becoming jobless, homeless, or bankrupt. Of course, those are extreme cases. In most negotiations, people have a few alternatives that may not be ideal, but they're tolerable.

> You always have a BATNA. What you're saying is that you don't *like* your BATNA. It's unattractive to you. But you have one.

To get back to the friend. His BATNA was to extend his job search in a probabilistic fashion. He chose not to accept company X's offer because he was optimistic that some Company Y would eventually make him a better offer.

Similarly, a home seller may reject a lowball offer from an uncooperative buyer in the hope that the future will bring a better offer.

Finally, to return to hotel negotiation: If my negotiations with the Holiday Inn had not resulted in an offer that was more attractive than what the Comfort Inn offered me, I would have walked away from the table.

10

It's alive! Constantly improve your BATNA

Think of your BATNA as a beloved plant or pet: You feed it, you water it. BATNAs need care and attention to thrive. If you stop nurturing them, they die.

Your BATNA is in a constant state of flux. It ebbs and flows. Whatever you do, don't be passive about it. For example, a home buyer might have three offers on her house today. Great BATNA, you might think. But three days from now, the inspection may go badly for one buyer, another buyer may not get the company transfer he anticipated and withdraw, and the third may find a more attractive house. So, now the seller's BATNAs have withered. In this situation, I would advise the seller to schedule an open house, place a full-color ad in the city newspaper, and move ahead with a touch-up paint job. Even if a seller has three offers in hand, it's wise to keep playing the field until the deal is signed, sealed, and delivered.

I've seen too many negotiators release their BATNAs before the proverbial cat is in the proverbial bag. A home buyer might fall in love with the second house she sees and refuse to view any others. A job recruiter might cancel all remaining interviews once the first candidate meets the bar. Prematurely releasing your BATNA dramatically reduces your power.

Prematurely releasing your BATNA dramatically reduces your power.

The surest way to improve your outcome and leverage your power better in any negotiation is to increase your BATNA's attractiveness. For example, to start a bidding war, a seller might have several buyers compete for his product or service. Similarly, a new car buyer might pit several sellers against one another, asking each to meet or beat the others' prices.

Having said this, I do not advocate starting bidding wars. It creates ill will when negotiators use their BATNAs in a threatening fashion. What to do instead? First, list your options in order of attractiveness. Suppose you're a job candidate and four companies have made you offers: Company W, Company X, Company Y, and Company Z. So far, you like Company W the most, but the other options are close behind. As tempting as it may be to start a bidding war, I would avoid it. Rather, I advise approaching Company W and saying something like,

It creates ill will when negotiators use their BATNAs in a threatening fashion.

If you give me an offer that has A, B, and C in it, I will accept immediately without asking for anything else. But if you're unable to offer me these terms, I'll need more time to decide. Please understand that I would still be interested in the offer and may decide to accept it.

What I like about this strategy is that the counterparty is reassured that you are not going to start a bidding war and that she can close the deal right now with you.

The best way of improving your BATNA is to fully explore all possible courses of action.

For example, think back to the friend who had the suboptimal job offer from Company X. He might list his alternatives as follows.

- Continue the job search. (I learned that my friend had second-round interviews at two companies, was short-listed at three more, and had other interviews scheduled. Based on this, he figured there was an 80 percent chance he'd have a job offer from another company within three weeks.)

- Work for a professor on a temporary basis. (He had a written invitation from an accounting professor to work on a short-term project that was not high-paying but rewarding and prestigious.)

- Flip burgers. (This may sound like a joke, but everyone should be open to several courses of action.)

The friend ranked his alternatives in order of attractiveness (utility to him). Of all the options, he was most keen about extending his formal job search and decided to focus on his upcoming job interviews.

Skilled negotiators always keep their alternatives open and attempt to improve upon them.

TRUTH

11

Don't reveal your BATNA

"Why is it so bad to reveal my BATNA?" you may ask. Once you reveal your BATNA, the other party has no incentive to offer you any more than your BATNA. Consider the following scenario:

Home seller: "My house is listed at $250,000. Another buyer has made an offer, but it's only for $175,000, which is too low. I'd like you to offer something in the range of $225,000 to $240,000."

Homebuyer: "Your house is lovely. However, I have my own financial needs to consider. I'll make you a cash offer of $176,000, and we can close at your convenience."

If you sensed something wrong with the home seller's approach, you're right: The seller revealed the BATNA to the other party. What's more, the BATNA was relatively unattractive. Once the homebuyer knows this information, she has absolutely no incentive to offer the seller anything but the bare minimum over the seller's BATNA, as illustrated in this example. Once you reveal your BATNA, the counterparty has you over a barrel.

Rest assured that other parties will seek information about your BATNA in a million different ways. They will prod you, quiz you, and taunt you. It's best to think of yourself as a CIA agent who has taken an oath never to reveal your BATNA, lest it compromise the nation's security.

> Once you reveal your BATNA, the counterparty has you over a barrel.

Are there special cases in which it makes sense to reveal your BATNA? I can only think of two.

- The eleventh hour is at hand, and negotiations are at a standstill. You've spent all day negotiating and gotten nowhere. If you don't reach an agreement, you'll miss your flight home. Before you walk out the door, you might consider revealing your BATNA. There's a chance the other party may meet it or beat it.

- You have a fantastic BATNA and would be happy simply to have the counterparty match or trivially improve upon it. But if you choose to reveal your BATNA, understand one thing: You're not going to get an offer significantly more attractive than it from any rational other party.

It's best to think of yourself as a CIA agent who has taken an oath never to reveal your BATNA, lest it compromise the nation's security.

These situations are truly rare. If you're like me, you don't want the other party to simply meet your BATNA—you want him to think it's much more attractive than it really is, so he'll make you a much better offer. So, don't share your BATNA unless you absolutely have to. And, even then, proceed carefully.

TRUTH

12

Don't lie about your BATNA

Your BATNA is your key source of bargaining power. And I've strictly cautioned you against revealing your BATNA. These may add up to a common temptation: Why not lie about your BATNA to claim a larger slice of the bargaining pie?

For instance, suppose I concoct a plan for getting a hefty raise: I plan to tell my boss that I have an amazing offer from another employer (this is a complete lie) and that to keep me, she must meet or beat it. Now, you try to talk me out of this deceitful plan!

You might try to talk me out of this plan by saying, "You'll surely ruin your reputation if you lie. It's a small world, and your boss will probably find out that you're lying. She'll never trust you again. You'll lose all respect at work." "Isn't it important to have some integrity?" "How would you like it if someone lied to you that way? Wouldn't you want to fire him?"

Okay, I'm beginning to see the light. Trying to bilk my boss sounds like a stinker of an idea from this ethical standpoint.

Are there any more reasons not to carry out my plan?

You might say, "Suppose your boss calls your bluff and says, 'Congratulations on the offer. We're proud of you and will miss you. I'm sure you'll enjoy your new job.'"

Oh dear, you're right again. If I lie about my BATNA, the counterparty might call my bluff, and then I would have one heck of a face-saving act to perform: "Uh, well, boss, I haven't quite decided to take the offer, and come to think of it, my kids really like the schools here...and I don't want to go through the trauma of a move. So never mind."

Okay, you've almost convinced me not to lie. Any additional arguments?

At this point, you say, "Are you aware that lying about a material fact is prosecutable?" You show me the legal code on this and explain that if my boss enters into an agreement based upon a material fact that I have knowingly misrepresented, I can be sued.

In sum, there are three darn good reasons to never lie about your BATNA.

There are three darn good reasons to never lie about your BATNA.

- **Ethical/moral**—You don't want to behave this way because it implicitly encourages others to behave similarly, which creates a corrupt society. Plus you'll ruin your reputation.

- **Strategic face-saving**—Just as in poker, someone can call your bluff at any time. In negotiation, there are many more "tells," or signs that someone's lying.

- **Legal/contractual**—Lying about a material fact (such as claiming that you have another job offer or offer on your house that you do not in fact possess) is a criminal act that may result in prosecution or a lawsuit.

TRUTH

13

Signal your BATNA

You may have noticed a BATNA-related Catch-22: "I can't tell the truth without being totally duped, and I can't lie without suffering moral-strategic-legal costs. What exactly do you advise?"

To make matters worse, counterparties often ask you about your BATNA directly. "Do you have any offers yet?" Similarly, a homebuyer asks home sellers, "Any action on your home?" And a vendor might bait a procurement director with, "Do you have another source for this product?"

So, what should you do when hit with a "What's-your-BATNA" question?

First, there are two things you shouldn't do.

- Don't ignore the question and hope it will go away. It won't.
- Don't turn the question around by saying, "I'll show you mine if you show me yours."

Rather, signal to the other party that you have a BATNA, without revealing it: "If you're inquiring about whether I have alternative courses of action, the answer is yes. But I'm sure you can understand why I can't discuss those with you at this time."

Here's another strategy that I even like better, in the context of an interested company asking a job-seeker how many job offers she has:

> ## Signal to the other party that you have a BATNA, without revealing it.

"I put an 80 percent probability of my having an offer from a *Fortune 100* firm in the next two weeks. I have three second-round interviews. I am on the short list at eight companies. And I have two phone interviews this week and five recruiting events coming up."

Reading between the lines, it's clear that this job-seeker does not have another job offer in hand, but she is signaling that her BATNA is being actively watered and fertilized and is blossoming wildly. Of course, I advocate saying these things only if they're true. This again points out the importance of not releasing your alternatives prematurely. Even if you get a tempting job offer, keep interviewing and attending recruiting events!

Even if you get a tempting job offer, keep interviewing and attending recruiting events!

The good thing about signaling is that saying things like, "I put an X percent chance on event Y happening" is not a material fact. It is a subjective probability.

Don't signal your BATNA to threaten the other party. Rather, send signals under the following conditions.

- The counterparty challenges you directly. ("Do you have any other job offers?")

- The counterparty is severely underestimating your alternatives.

- The counterparty is working with false information about you that you want to set straight.

- The counterparty has been lowballing you, and you wish to signal that he needs to increase the value of his proposals quickly.

TRUTH

14

Research the other party's BATNA

If your feet are the key source of your bargaining power in a negotiation, bear in mind that the other party has feet, too.

It's surprising to me how little research negotiators do on the other party. Negotiators become so self-absorbed with their own BATNAs that they often fail to think strategically about who's on the other side of the table. This is even more perplexing when there is good data available, often publicly, about the other party.

If your feet are the key source of your bargaining power in a negotiation, bear in mind that the other party has feet, too.

In my first job, I was earning a rather low salary. "It's okay—I'm doing what really counts," I would tell myself. Fortunately, a fellow employee hinted to me that I might be underpaid. Salaries are a matter of public information at state or federal jobs. So I went to the library and spent several hours finding out exactly what everyone was paid. Then I did some further analysis of salaries based on gender, years of experience, field of study, and so on. Using the information, I made charts and graphs and plotted myself on them among several comparison points including performance. Then I made an appointment with my boss. I got a raise in less than two weeks.

If you don't research your case, you may falsely assume the other party's BATNA is better than it is, which puts you in a position of weakness. Moreover, if you focus just on your own BATNA, you get anchored by it. Even if you don't uncover relevant data about the other party's BATNA, thinking about the other person's BATNA dramatically improves your outcome.[7]

Here are the big five DO's and DON'Ts when it comes to BATNAs.

- DON'T reveal your BATNA, except under special conditions.
- DO as much research as possible on the other party's BATNA.
- DON'T engage in bidding wars, but DO make constant attempts to improve your BATNA.
- DON'T lie about your BATNA.
- DO signal to the other party that you have valuable alternative options.

15

Develop your reservation price

A few years ago, I was selling my house. I tried to practice what I preach in my classes: Develop an attractive BATNA, set a feasible target (aspiration point), and so on. But none of it changed the hard truth that I didn't have an offer on my house!

To make matters worse, I made the grave mistake of telling friends about my lack of success. From that point, they took daily delight in grilling me about the house: "Hey, what's your BATNA?" As the days dragged on and I still didn't have an offer, I'd hear things like, "I can loan you a good book!"

One day I arrived at work with a picture of drunk fraternity guys on my laptop screen. They were surrounded by empty bottles and other party paraphernalia. A murmur rippled through the office. Had I forgotten to change my screen saver after a wild spring break? Was I having a midlife crisis?

"Here's my BATNA," I announced solemnly. Blank looks. I explained that in the event that I didn't get an offer on my house, my next best course of action would be to rent it—to these party animals. I described the men in the picture as undergraduates taking all of their courses pass-fail. My coworkers were concerned: "Wouldn't these 'young men' destroy your house?" This led to a discussion about risk and the benefits of a damage deposit. Then more questions: "Are these guys going to agree to let you have realtors show the house?" That led to a discussion of the wisdom of securing a contractual agreement that would involve a clear understanding of certain hours during which the house could be shown. Then more discussion, about neighbors growing angry with loud music from the house, my name on the police blotter, and the like.

Even though BATNAs, just like the party animals, are messy, subjective, and psychological, we must be able to make them monetary; otherwise, we won't be able to compare alternatives meaningfully.

Finally, someone said, "So what's the least money I could offer you for your house now?" In short, what is the monetary equivalent of my BATNA? In other words, even though BATNAs, just like the party animals, are messy, subjective, and psychological, we must be able to make them monetary; otherwise, we won't be able to compare alternatives meaningfully.

Given that I put a value on subjective-emotional things such as my time, peace of mind, marital harmony, neighborly relations, liquid assets, and absence of conflicts, I came up with a number. A penny less meant that I would rather rent than sell. A penny more meant that I would rather sell than rent. That indifference point is my *reservation price.* It's what negotiators mean by their "bottom line."

A different person selling the same house with my same BATNA might have a different reservation point because they have a different value system, different risk psychology, and so on.

Thus, the beauty of a reservation point is that it quantifies subjective values.

The lesson: After you identify your BATNA, convert it to a reservation point.

After you identify your BATNA, convert it to a reservation point.

Recall my friend who was looking for a job. Say he determined the least amount of money that company X could offer him such that he would be indifferent to accepting the offer versus declining it and extending his job search. That go-no-go number would be his reservation point.

TRUTH

16

Beware of ZOPA myopia

Now, let's put together what you've learned so far. If I have a BATNA, so do you. If I have a reservation point, so do you. The $64 million dollar question (inflation), then, is whether there's a positive overlap between my reservation point and yours.

The *bargaining zone* represents the overlap (or lack thereof) between your reservation point and mine. The *zone of possible agreement*, or ZOPA, represents the overlap between the most the buyer is willing to pay and the least the seller is willing to accept.

I always think of ZOPAs like a "dance floor." I envision two negotiators dancing, each trying to lead the other to his reservation point. It's possible that there's no space on the dance floor, meaning that the maximum a buyer is willing to pay is less than the minimum a seller will accept. It's also possible that the dance floor is the size of a football field.

> The *zone of possible agreement*, or ZOPA, represents the overlap between the most the buyer is willing to pay and the least the seller is willing to accept.

The most common mistake people make is to assume the bargaining zone is much smaller than it actually is. I call this *ZOPA myopia*. ZOPA myopia often occurs because people are anchored by their own reservation prices.

Most of the time we never learn the true size of the ZOPA. However, people often feel "buyer's remorse" when their opening offer is accepted happily. Similarly, sellers often feel regret when their asking prices are immediately paid in cash by buyers. To get a sense of the bargaining zone, consider the example of a professional speaker. On behalf of a large association, I asked the speaker what he would charge to appear at the association's annual meeting. The speaker told me he was willing to do the engagement for as little as $10,000, but he desired $15,000. Thus, I knew the speaker's reservation price and his desirable price. I tested the speaker regarding his reservation point: Would he really walk away from this deal if the potential client offered $9,500? He said he would.

To make our analysis come alive, suppose we have the same information on the hiring company. The company hoped to pay the speaker $5,000 for the engagement but was actually willing to pay up to $12,000, given that it wanted to confirm the meeting schedule within the next 48 hours.

The following represents the ZOPA, or the overlap in parties' reservation prices:

$4,000 $6,000 $8,000 $10,000 $12,000 $14,000 $16,000

ZOPA = $2,000

In this example, the ZOPA is positive; there is a $2,000 overlap. However, there is a negative overlap in the *demands* the parties are making, with the speaker requesting $15,000 and the hiring company proposing $5,000. But the real action of negotiation is in what's left unsaid: the parties' reservation prices.

Obviously, the speaker would like to know that the hiring firm would be willing to pay $12,000; and, of course, the hiring firm would like to know the speaker's reservation price. But neither party is going to openly reveal its reservation point.

Of course, no one, save a neutral mediator or third party, would ever have perfect information about the counterparty's reservation price, but the point remains: There is a dance floor, and it often makes sense for two parties to tango their way to a deal, rather than exercising their BATNAs.

17

Set optimistic but realistic aspirations

While having a BATNA is important, the risk is that you become so focused on your BATNAs and reservation points that you settle for the first deal better than your BATNA or above your reservation point. Instead, you should hold out for a much more attractive deal, one closer to your aspiration point.

Your BATNA tells you when to *walk*, not when to *sign*.

If you accept the first proposal that exceeds your BATNA, you have fallen victim to the "underaspiring" negotiator syndrome. The primary symptom: You feel great about

Your BATNA tells you when to *walk*, not when to *sign*.

getting a deal. You perceive the bargaining zone as small and thus feel lucky just to have reached an agreement. However, when you later realize the *actual* size of the bargaining zone, your excitement may melt into disappointment.

What you need is an *aspiration point*. An aspiration point represents the monetary equivalent of your ideal set of terms. Suppose you are selling your house. You might tell me your reservation price is $250,000 (and your house is listed at $275,000). I would ask you if that represents a favorable set of terms. I want you to be optimistic, but realistic. You may say then that $275,000 would be attractive and realistic because that's what houses with similar features and floorplans have sold for in your neighborhood. That's your aspiration point! The person you negotiate with will have, whether she knows it or not, an aspiration point, too. That's why it's important that you know yours.

You need to develop your aspiration point *before* going into negotiation. It's not enough to hope to do well. Nor is it enough to hope to get well above your BATNA. I'm also not a fan of aspiration "ranges." Ranges are wishy-washy; they have diminished anchoring potential and, not surprisingly, the counterparty tends to hear only the part of your range closest to *her* aspiration point (the lowest price you're willing to sell for). So, it's essential to develop an actual aspiration point—I call it a *target*—for the negotiation. Not to have and to know your aspiration point is like going into a negotiation with a defense but no offense.

But you can also go too far with your aspirations. You could develop wildly unrealistic aspiration points. The danger of developing an outlandish target is that it can create the chilling *effect* in the counterparty and set you up for disappointment.

The chilling effect occurs when an opening offer is so insulting that the counterparty doesn't even care to respond because he doesn't want to acknowledge it. Suppose, for example, that a buyer makes a $100,000 offer on your $275,000 home. You wouldn't even want to give that buyer the courtesy of a response. That's the chilling effect. The polar opposite of the chilling effect is the *winner's curse*. If you immediately and gleefully accept my first offer, that tells me my offer was too generous. You should not accept the first offer above your reservation price.

> Suppose, for example, that a buyer makes a $100,000 offer on your $275,000 home. You wouldn't even want to give that buyer the courtesy of a response. That's the chilling effect.

Here are the aspiration point DOs:

- DO think about the other party's BATNA. You don't know what it is, of course, but you can still think about it. As it turns out, if you were to develop an aspiration point that was exactly equivalent to the other party's BATNA/reservation point, that would be a great opening offer to make.

- DO seek comparison data and focus on points that are most favorable to you (like you would do if you researched the salaries or fees earned by people with similar qualifications and experience to yours).

- DO follow these basic steps.

  1. Identify your key goals.

  2. Brainstorm your options.

  3. Plan your opening move.

Your aspiration should be such that if you proposed your terms and the other party immediately accepted, you would still feel good.

Here are the DON'Ts:

- DON'T use your BATNA as a starting point and then dial it up or down to arrive at a target point. You can't derive your aspiration from a BATNA-based formula.
- DON'T state an outrageous aspiration that you can't back up with data (comparables).
- DON'T withhold your aspiration until the other party has spoken.
- DON'T state a range of aspiration points.

TRUTH

18

Plan your concessions

Few negotiations end in one round. Rather, there is a back and forth, with parties making offers and counteroffers. This is the dance of negotiation. I advise you to plot your offers and counteroffers with the precision that a football coach would bring to the Super Bowl. In other words, to prepare for an upcoming negotiation, you should know every stat about past negotiations: how many concessions you made, the size of your average concession, how many concessions the other party made, how far apart the two opening offers were, and so on.

Why? Because people often get carried away by the momentum of the negotiation and fail to think analytically about the pattern of concessions. This leads to one or more of the following mistakes.

> **Plot your offers and counteroffers with the precision that a football coach would bring to the Super Bowl.**

■ You make concessions too quickly, before you explore interests.

■ You make concessions that are too large. (In contrast, making small concessions creates goodwill and signals that you're reasonable, but getting closer to your reservation price.)

■ You make concessions while the other party remains intransigent.

To get in the habit of keeping track of the negotiation game, I strongly advise keeping a little notepad in front of you, even make visual sketches, rather than writing in paragraphs. That way, you can say things like,

Look Pat, I want to point out that I've come down $50,000 since we started talking, and by my records you've increased your offer by only $10,000 so far, or only one-fifth of what I've come down. (Such a statement puts pressure on the counterparty to make concessions.)

Francis, I've made concessions on all the issues we're talking about; according to my records, you've only made concessions on one. I ask you now to consider what you could do on some of the other issues.

Sometimes, negotiators make a plan they can't follow through on. For example, I've heard several negotiators plan to make no concessions. This is ill advised: If you refuse to make concessions, the negotiation quickly reaches a stalemate.

Sometimes, negotiators make the opposite mistake: They open with a great first offer, which is inevitably refused by the counterparty. On their next move, they make a too-deep concession, effectively giving up all their bargaining ground.

As a general principle, negotiators should make concessions on issues that are the least important to them. Don't expect the other side to give you credit for making a concession. They usually won't. For this reason, you need to announce your concession. Something like,

I've been listening to you carefully. My current offer on the issue of paid vacation days is seven per year. I know you want that number to be higher. So, I have thought about it and I could live with 10 paid vacation days per year. (Get up and cross out 7 and write 10). Thus, I'm willing to concede on this issue by increasing from 7 to 10 days.

Note that in the preceding statement, the negotiator is doing four things: (1) reminding the counterparty of an opening offer of seven days; (2) drawing attention to the fact of being willing to make a concession on that issue; (3) writing the new number on the board, another way to create quid pro quo pressure; (4) explicitly inviting the other party to respond.

If you don't invite the counterparty to respond, he has much less incentive to make a concession.

I would advise you as the negotiator in this scenario not to make further concessions on any of the issues until the counterparty has made a concession. When making concessions, if the counterparty doesn't write down the numbers proposed, take over the board

If the counterparty doesn't write down the numbers proposed, take over the board yourself.

yourself. I've seen too many negotiations break down because of "miscommunication." Words and proposals fly back and forth, but everyone gets confused when it comes to actually writing the exact terms.

Suppose the counterparty does indeed make a concession. At this point, you might want to make another concession—again on an issue that is less important to you. I advise negotiators to reduce the size of their concessions with each successive concession, to signal to the counterparty that they are nearing their reservation point.

TRUTH

19

Be aware of the "even-split" ploy

The following interchange actually occurred. What, if anything, is wrong with this picture?

Party A: I'll offer you $15M to buy your company.

Party B: Are you kidding? It's worth much more than that, and I have several offers. I would want at least $47M.

Party A: That's a lot more than I'd ever want to spend. The most I could offer would be $18M.

Party B: Well, then we probably won't reach a deal, because the company is worth $47M. But I might agree to $46M.

Party A: Still unacceptable. My highest bid would be $22M. But that would have to be with a closing in the next 30 days.

Party B: I don't think I could accept that offer. I'm not trying to drive a hard bargain, but I think we both realize this company is special. I would agree to $45M.

Party A: My final offer is $25M.

Party B: Okay, I have an idea. Why don't we just split the difference, for an even $35M? That would be fair to both of us.

Party A: That sounds fair, I guess.

Upon first glance, three things jump out about this negotiation.

First, the party's opening offers of $15M and $47M are wildly apart. There is a divide of $32M. That's not atypical.

Second, both parties make concessions in a somewhat quid pro quo fashion. That's advisable, per the previous Truth. However, I would encourage Party A to invite another concession from Party B, because Party A made three concessions, while Party B made two concessions.

> It's almost inevitable that one negotiator will suggest "splitting the difference."

70

However, the real problem for Party A is not the *number* of concessions she made, but the *magnitude* of those concessions. Party A made concessions of a depth of $10M (initial offer of $15M, and most recent offer of $25M). In contrast, Party B made concessions one-fifth of that depth, or $2M (initial starting offer of $47M and most recent offer of $45M). Party A will probably never recover from this blunder.

It's almost inevitable that one negotiator will suggest "splitting the difference" to close the gap. The emotional appeal of this ploy is overwhelming for most fair-minded negotiators, to that point that it seems selfish and egotistical to refuse. The problem in the previous negotiation is that Party A made much deeper concessions than Party B. Yet when Party B suggests splitting the difference, it's as if the past never occurred.

This is why I strongly caution negotiators to carefully plan their concessions. In our rush to wrap up negotiations and show good faith, we often make concessions that are too steep and quick.

> In our rush to wrap up negotiations and show good faith, we often make concessions that are too steep and quick.

TRUTH

20

The pregame

Negotiations have a beginning, middle, and end. If we think about the golf analogy, there is a beginning, in which the players (golfers) socialize and maybe even talk about the rules for engagement. There is the game itself (9 or 18 holes). And then there is the postgame, at which time socializing might occur or the golfers might discuss the game.

Obviously, there will be dramatic variations in the "negotiation game" across different cultures. For example, in her book *Tough Choices: A Memoir*, Carly Fiorina, CEO of Hewlett-Packard from 1999 to 2005, talks about the pregame in her negotiations with Korean company Lucky GoldStar. The pregame consisted of a traditional Korean barbeque at which Carly was given a lovely female escort and several rounds of scotch for several hours. The actual negotiation began the next day. Fiorina said that partaking in the pregame was essential to build a foundation for the actual negotiation. Had she refused to be part of Lucky GoldStar's pregame, the negotiation would not have been successful.

The pregame begins when negotiators meet one another and exchange pleasantries. (Some cultures and companies like Korea's Lucky GoldStar have elaborate rituals.) The game begins when one party starts talking about the issues at hand. The negotiation ends when the deal is signed or when someone walks out. The postgame refers to the conversation and rituals that take place after the deal is signed.

> The pregame begins when negotiators meet one another and exchange pleasantries.

I have strongly advised negotiators to make the first offer or make an immediate counteroffer. This advice might imply that you should immediately launch your offer into the negotiation airspace.

I don't suggest that your offer should be the first words out of your mouth. It is important to engage in proper pregame activities.

People from other cultures differ with respect to the format of the pregame activities. Spend anywhere from the first 5 to 20 minutes engaging in relationship-focused talk. Some call it schmoozing. Others call it small talk. Still others call it B.S. Whatever it is, it works.

Some call it schmoozing. Others call it small talk. Still others call it B.S. Whatever it is, it works.

What's more, scientific data indicates that negotiators who engage in as little as five minutes of schmoozing are more successful than negotiators who immediately get down to business. *Schmoozing* is any type of conversation that does not have to do with the negotiation at hand.[8] It creates more trust.

At some point, schmoozing needs to end and the game of negotiation needs to be played. The transition from pleasantries to offers can be abrupt, so it is important to signal that you are about to make a conversational sea change. Signal that you are getting ready to refocus the discussion by uttering one of the following statements.

■ Shall we get down to business?

■ I understand you've got a plane to catch, so I don't want to dilly-dally. I've prepared a set of terms for your consideration.

■ I've thought about the business deal, and I'm wondering if this is a good time to turn our focus to that.

■ What are your time constraints? I know that I have to be on my way at 5 p.m., so I think we should begin.

TRUTH

21

The game

Most people don't have trouble initiating small talk because they do it all the time. However, they often have not taken lessons in negotiation, so they don't know where to begin. You may wonder, "Who should begin?" That's a strategic decision on your part.

Some negotiations are heavily scripted, meaning that rules, norms, and codes of conduct exist. For example, house selling in the United States usually occurs with a seller listing her home. The seller's list price is her first offer. The buyer usually will make an offer through an agent, and in most states that is a written offer.

Buying a car is a scripted negotiation. The sticker price is the seller's first offer. The buyer makes a first offer, usually verbally. I would counsel buyers to make first offers in writing. They have more oomph.

Other negotiations are less scripted, and you have more degrees of freedom. When people are unsure of what to do, they often become passive. That is strategically unwise. If you are concerned that there is a process that you should be following but that you are unaware of and you are worried about making a faux pas, I strongly advise doing the following.

- Ask experts who have negotiated in that domain. For example, if your interest is in price negotiation for bulk buying for a store or chain or stores, you might interview the designated person at a store or business serving businesses near you who routinely does that. She can tell you what to expect.

- If you do not have experts in that domain to consult, ask the other party if his company has a certain procedure.

- Announce that you are unsure of how to begin, but you will make your best attempt.

Just because the pleasantries have ended and the negotiators are anxious to get down to the business of negotiating, make sure that you can answer yes to all of the questions that follow. If you can't, don't negotiate yet.

- In a job negotiation, have you been offered the job? Many negotiators begin negotiating before they have a job offer. Don't get roped into negotiations before you have been offered a job. You are at your apex of bargaining power when you have been offered a job but haven't accepted it yet.

> Don't get roped into negotiations before you have been offered a job. You are at your apex of bargaining power when you have been offered a job but haven't accepted it yet.

- Does the counterparty have the authority to make a deal, or is that person simply collecting information to convey to a person of real authority? This is the problem that often gets car buyers in trouble: They negotiate with slick-talking sales people who do not have authority or who claim to not have authority. Only negotiate with people who have the authority to make deals without consultation from other superiors.

- Ask the counterparty if she is prepared to negotiate or whether she is merely collecting information. I often get calls from companies that are collecting information about speakers, such as how they work and what their process is. Eventually, they ask me about price, but I don't answer their question. I say that once they are interested in talking details about their engagement and have narrowed the field, I would want to set aside the time to talk to them. One of my favorite sentences is, "I want to give this discussion the attention it deserves and not speak off of the top of my head."

> Only negotiate with people who have the authority to make deals without consultation from other superiors.

TRUTH

22

The postgame

Can you imagine inviting a guest to a dinner party who shows up, walks in the door, sits at the dining room table, eats, and then leaves? That would be absurd. You would expect that the invited guest would socialize with you before as well as after the meal.

Usually, negotiators get the point of socializing before the negotiation. But, often, they truncate the conversation and immediately leave. Negotiation etiquette dictates beginnings, middles, and ends.

Successful postgames should serve two purposes in negotiation:

- Cementing the deal (making it hard or impossible for parties to retract agreed-upon deals)
- Paving the way for future relationships

Howard Raiffa gives one postgame piece of advice in his book *The Art and Science of Negotiation*: "Don't gloat."[9] Negotiators who gloat only cause ill will in the counterparty and often risk that the other party will retract the deal or at least not consummate his end of the bargain.

Gloating can be a disaster, at least in terms of how negotiators feel about the deal. The other party is prone to feel disappointed, unhappy, and less successful. That can lead to payback, now or the next time you negotiate with that party. You are liable to receive harsh or at least less generous treatment in a subsequent negotiation. Send a courtesy note 24 hours postgame via email or snail mail saying that you enjoyed meeting with the other party and are happy that you will be working together on this deal. The other important aspect of the postgame is to cement the deal. If the negotiation terms have not been written down and signed jointly, take the initiative of writing down the terms yourself and circulating them to the parties involved.

> If the negotiation terms have not been written down and signed jointly, take the initiative of writing down the terms yourself and circulating them to the parties involved.

In the event that the postgame ended in an impasse (no deal), resist the urge to verbally punish the other party or act out. Remember, you are an ambassador for your company. And you might find yourself at the table again with this counterparty sooner than you think, especially if your best alternative to negotiated agreement (BATNA) suddenly deteriorates. So, as a general principle, assume the world is small, and help everyone "save face" (preserve dignity).

My favorite sentence is this: "I know we did not see eye to eye on this, but I respect your views."

TRUTH

23

What does "win-win" really mean?

Almost everyone is familiar with the idea of a "win-win negotiation." Seasoned negotiators will tell you that the only good negotiation is one that ends in a win-win. Yet some people think that simply means reaching any agreement. Other people think it's a negotiation that leaves all parties still speaking. Still others think win-win means dividing everything equally down the middle. Although all of these outcomes are desirable, none of them captures the central concept of a win-win negotiation.

Simply put, a win-win negotiation is a negotiated outcome in which parties have reached an agreement that cannot be mutually improved upon. Thus, the term "win-win negotiation" actually reflects an important economic concept: Win-win solutions lie on what economists refer to as the Pareto Optimal Frontier, after the Italian economist Vilfredo Pareto.

Pareto's litmus test was simple: If there is no way to improve upon the agreement from the standpoint of either party, the negotiators have reached the Pareto Optimal Frontier. However, if there is another agreement that both parties would prefer or that one party prefers and the other is indifferent to, the negotiators have suboptimized, failing to reach the Pareto Optimal Frontier. When this happens, I call it a "lose-lose agreement." If it's that simple, why don't negotiators just aim for an agreement on the Pareto Optimal Frontier? One big problem: In most negotiations, neither party is going to express what he truly wants, so there's no clear way of seeing the Frontier's boundaries. How, then, do negotiators have any clue that they are on the Frontier?

> Simply put, a win-win negotiation is a negotiated outcome in which parties have reached an agreement that cannot be mutually improved upon.

Unfortunately, they don't always know. But there are multiple clear symptoms of a suboptimal outcome for a given negotiation:

- Your first offer was accepted immediately by the other party.
- You made an offer, the other party counter-offered, and then you agreed to split the difference.
- You and the other party considered less than five potential deals.
- You didn't ask the other party any questions.
- The other party didn't ask you any questions.
- Neither party tried to "tweak" the deal to improve it.
- You revealed nothing to the other party.
- The other party revealed nothing to you.
- You negotiated only one issue (such as price).
- You negotiated more than one issue, but you negotiated each independently of the others.

If your deal is characterized by three or more of these symptoms, there is a very good chance you suboptimized and ended up with a lose-lose deal. Fortunately, you can do several things to make sure you never end up on the "lose-lose frontier" again.

The following Truth presents an in-depth look at the factors that lead to suboptimal agreements, along with several of the strategies you can use to avoid them.

TRUTH

24

Satisficing versus optimizing

Reaching true win-win agreements is not easy. More often than not, from an objective perspective, you can spot a deal that both parties would like more—often dramatically more—than the one they agreed to. This means that both parties settled for less than they should have.

Consider the case introduced in Truth 6 of two sisters and the single orange. One of the sisters wants to drink all the juice from the orange, while the other wants the whole peel to make scones. Instead of being clear about what they want, they both made the same demand: "I want the orange." They finally split the orange in half. One sister drinks the juice from her half and throws out the peel; the other sister uses the peel from her half and discards the juice. Managers and executives often reach outcomes tantamount to cutting oranges in half. They are oblivious to the existence of another feasible agreement that would have been far more beneficial, just as the sisters would have been much better off by splitting the orange into juice and peel!

That brings us to a key question: Why do people settle so willingly for lose-lose agreements? There are three main reasons:

- Satisficing
- Lack of feedback
- The fixed-pie perception

Satisficing

Nobel Laureate Herb Simon coined the term satisficing for the human tendency to suboptimize—to work just enough to achieve a mediocre goal. Simon contrasted satisificing with a much more productive behavior: optimizing.

First and foremost, negotiators just plain set their sights too low.

One early satisficing experiment[10] asked people to multiply $1 \times 2 \times 3 \times 4 \times 5 \times 6 \times 7 \times 8$. Most people tackled this by multiplying the first few numbers and then making an educated guess at the answer. However, on average, their answers were way too low. A different group was given the same numbers to multiply, but in reverse order: $8 \times 7 \times 6 \times 5 \times 4 \times 3 \times 2 \times 1$. This group made better guesses, but their answers were still totally wrong. The results indicate that people rely excessively on mental shortcuts and take "cognitive naps" that can result in costly mistakes. In other words, people are lazy.

Another study compared the negotiations of spouses and dating couples to those between strangers.[11] It seems reasonable to guess that married and dating couples, presumably interested in nurturing a long-term relationship, would reach the most win-win outcomes. They didn't. Complete strangers had a greater incidence of win-win outcomes than couples! Why? Satisficing. On average, the couples quickly settled for the first set of tolerable terms. In contrast, the strangers were more inclined to think about their ultimate aspirations and explore more routes to achieving these. This optimizing led to more win-win agreements.

> People rely excessively on mental shortcuts and take "cognitive naps" that can result in costly mistakes.

Lack of Feedback

A second reason people fail to reach win-win deals is that they simply don't get feedback about their agreements. Thus, most people have no objective idea about the outcome of their negotiation. As a result, their behavior becomes self-reinforcing. This is akin to someone eating highly fatty foods, never exercising, never checking her blood pressure, and proudly concluding, "I'm not dead, so my blood pressure must be healthy." This person is operating without knowledge of her actual health and, more importantly, what she could do to maximize it. I strongly encourage everyone to seek opportunities to put their negotiation skills to the test—by seeking feedback.

The Fixed-Pie Perception

A third reason for lose-lose agreements is related to the "fixed-pie perception," or the nearly universal belief that one's own interests are diametrically opposed to those of the other party.[12] It epitomizes the win-lose type of thinking that marks most negotiations. If I believe that you are wholly opposed to whatever I want, we don't have much opportunity to create a win-win deal.

Many people falsely believe that the other party has preferences that are directly opposed to their own on all dimensions, when in fact this isn't true.

You will encounter an alarmingly high incidence of fixed-pie perceptions, since many people falsely believe that the other party has preferences that are directly opposed to their own on all dimensions, when in fact this isn't true.[13] In the instance of the Orange Sisters, it would be akin to the first sister swearing that her sibling also wanted the juice when what the second sister truly wanted was the peel.

So, if you go the way of the odds as confirmed by research, chances are you are headed toward a lose-lose negotiation scenario. The next Truths explore how to reach win-win outcomes.

TRUTH

25

There are really only two kinds of negotiations

There are two basic kinds of negotiations: fixed-sum and variable-sum.

In fixed-sum negotiations, the parties' interests are directly opposed, such that however much one gains, the other loses, and vice versa. Suppose you and I are negotiating over price. I'm the buyer and you're the seller. My reservation point is $80, but I'm obviously not going to tell you that. Your reservation point is $60, but you would rather be hit by lightning than volunteer that.

I start the negotiation by offering low ("I'll pay you $25"), to which you counter high ("Nothing less than $120!"), and each of us continues trying to get a better deal for ourselves. In the end, we are dividing a fixed sum of resources. The zone of possible agreement (ZOPA), no matter how you look at it, is always $20 (the difference between the $80 I'm secretly willing to pay and the $60 you're secretly willing to settle for).

0---10---20---30---40---50---60---70---80---90---100---110---120

←——————→

ZOPA

In variable-sum negotiations, the ZOPA can be expanded. For example, suppose that in the previous example, my reservation point is $80 for a cash deal, but I'm willing to pay $100 if you will accept credit. Your reservation point is $60 for cash but $70 for credit. If we just look at the ZOPA for the cash deal only, it is exactly $20 ($80 − $60 = $20). However, the ZOPA is $10 greater when we consider a credit deal ($100 − $70 = $30).

Single-issue negotiations are by definition fixed-sum negotiations. In the first example, if you and I are negotiating over price, then whatever I gain is your loss. And whatever you gain, I lose. However, if we can identify another negotiable issue that at least one of us cares about, we have created the potential for a win-win deal. We did this in the second example, when we separated the purchase price and the method of payment (cash or credit).

Many negotiations are disguised as single-issue. But negotiators can do two things to prevent these from becoming fixed-sum negotiations.

- Add an issue from outside the current negotiation's scope. ("Is your pet frog for sale, too?")

- Split the issue(s) at stake into multiple issues. ("What if I paid with credit?")

The process of identifying more than one negotiation issue is called unbundling.[14] By unbundling single-issue negotiations into multi-issue negotiations, negotiators create more opportunities for win-win trade-offs.

Consider a business scenario that initially looks like a fixed-sum negotiation. A company's sales force learns that the company's merger-and-acquisitions group wants to buy the sales force's best business-to-business customer. To either side, it may look like an either-or situation. But, as they discuss and unbundle the negotiation, they find other factors to add to the negotiation— expanded territories for the sales force, alternative targets for the M&A group, line-item budget and goal adjustments—and with the new issues carved out, they are able to reach a win-win agreement.

> By unbundling single-issue negotiations into multi-issue negotiations, negotiators create more opportunities for win-win trade-offs.

Many negotiators fail to unbundle issues because they look at the world myopically. Often this nearsightedness is around one issue: price. In fact, if you asked would-be negotiators about the three things most important to them, many would reply, "Price, price, and price." Price is important, of course, but even concerning price, there is the possibility of unbundling. This includes considering terms such as amount of down payment, interest rate, type of remuneration, or for that matter, volume discounts.

In summary, if there is truly just one issue, the negotiation will be fixed-sum by definition. But even in seemingly single-issue negotiations, identifying additional issues creates the potential to unbundle a fixed-sum negotiation into a variable-sum one. And that means potential for a win-win.

TRUTH

26

Ask triple-I questions

In a major technology transfer deal between two divisions of a large, diversified company, several million dollars of internal and external sales profits were at stake. Following is an excerpt from one of the negotiations this deal involved. Let's call this negotiator Chris.

> *Chris: George, time is becoming pressing, so I would like to propose my bottom-line offer, which I do truly believe is fair.*
>
> *As you can see, I have incorporated a number of concessions:*
>
> *(1) We will split development costs—that is, a net payment to you of $600K. (2) We will split all profits 50/50. We will also split all losses on this technology 50/50. I really cannot be fairer than this, and it assumes equal risk into the future. I have really tried to be fair and considerate to your position in this offer. I hope you will find the several concessions acceptable and that you agree this is fair all around.*

What is your first impression of this negotiator? Is Chris' focus on "fairness" creating potential for win-win?

Now, contrast that approach with the one that follows, made by a different person negotiating the same issue. Let's call this negotiator Saba.

> *Saba: Our estimates for profits from external sales of the technology are $12.0 million. We estimate that the internal market is $2 million. I think a fair deal in this case would be for us to pay you your development costs of $1.2 million, split the internal profits 50/50, and then give you 25 percent of the external profits. That would mean a total package for your department of $5.2 million. Please let me know if any of your estimates contradict any of the information above. What do you need to be comfortable? It would be helpful to have some idea of what you estimate that the impact of releasing the product into the market would do to your divisional sales. We don't want to hurt your sales too much, but I do not know what you expect the effect to be.*

What is your impression of this negotiator? Did you notice that

Saba asks several questions and shares her perceptions, consistently asking the other party for clarification?

The key difference in these negotiators' styles is that Saba asked many more questions than Chris, including those aimed at clarification. In fact, Chris did not ask a single question, but made a threat and several demands. Chris also imposes his view on the counterparty without seeking clarification. In contrast, Saba's combination of explicit and implicit questions (for example, "We don't want to hurt your sales too much, but I do not know what you expect the effect to be") elicited a counterparty response that included several pieces of valuable information. The information Saba uncovered allowed her to craft a response that was good for her own division and that of the counterparty. In contrast, Chris' bulldog approach led to escalating one-upmanship with the counterparty and an eventual stalemate.

Most negotiators don't ask enough questions. Not surprisingly, then, negotiators don't exchange a lot of information. Sharing information typically constitutes less than 10 percent of their total communication.[15] The other problem is that when negotiators do ask questions, they ask the wrong kinds of questions. For example, negotiators often ask intrusive questions about the other party's best alternative to a negotiated agreement (BATNA); these queries will not help the negotiators expand the pie. A good rule of thumb: Do not ask the other party a question you would be unwilling to answer yourself.

Win-win questions satisfy one or more of the "triple I" principles: interests, incentives, and inquiry.

In general, win-win questions satisfy one or more of the "triple I" principles: interests, incentives, and inquiry.

First and foremost, win-win questions elicit information about the underlying interests of the other party, rather than about their demands. For example, a landowner negotiating use of his land for pasture to a cattle rancher might ask, "Are water rights or alternative access routes to the pasture important to you?"

Second, win-win questions do not give other parties an incentive to lie or misrepresent themselves. If the cattle rancher asks how many cattle could feed and water on an average acre of the property owner's land, there is no incentive for the landowner to lie about a need for excessive rent.

Third, good win-win questions allow the other party to either confirm or refute. This type of question-asking is an inquiry, as opposed to advocacy. Negotiators, like Saba, who follow an inquiry mode are open to multiple outcomes, and they test hypotheses and predictions about which outcome would be win-win. Thus, inquiry-based negotiators ask questions much like a scientist would. The answers give them data to either refute or support their predictions.

TRUTH

27

Reveal your interests

Once you have sharpened your question-asking skills, you dramatically improve your chances of learning valuable information from the other party. But there is no guarantee that the other party will provide valuable answers to questions asked. They may not hear you, or more commonly, they may withhold information, fearing exploitation or vulnerability.

Just how big is the impact of revealing information on a negotiators' bottom line? Negotiators who provide information to the other party about their interests improve their outcomes, or profits, by over 10 percent.[16]

So, why is there so much reluctance among negotiators to reveal information? There are a few reasons. First, conventional negotiation wisdom holds that negotiators should maintain poker faces at all times. It is unfortunate that well-meaning colleagues and mentors have coached so many negotiators to conceal everything. This advice has led to a shrinking of the pie of resources under negotiation. Second, most people constrain their definitions of "information that could be revealed" to best alternative to a negotiated agreement (BATNA)–related information, rather than anything about their broader interests.

> Negotiators who provide information to the other party about their interests improve their outcomes, or profits, by over 10 percent.

Negotiators can reveal or "signal" their interests in several ways. Direct disclosure is one method; subtle signaling is another. All of the following statements can significantly expand the pie. Consider adding them to your negotiation vocabulary.

- "Issue X is more important to me than Y, but I care about both."
- "A 10 percent gain on issue X would be more valuable to me than a 10 percent gain on Y."
- "If I were to rank-order the issues' importance, X would be higher than Y."

Also consider adding the following questions to your negotiation vocabulary.

- "Which is more important to you: X or Y?"
- "What would give you more value: increasing X or Y?"
- "If I were to increase payment on X but decrease payment on Y, would that be better for you?"

A major benefit of revealing your interests is that you double that probability that the other party will disclose hers. This mirroring reflects the *reciprocity principle*. In studies on reciprocity, under normal conditions, the incidence of providing information to the other party is 19 percent. But when negotiators provide information to the other party, it jumps to 40 percent, based on the reciprocity principle. Keep in mind, however, that reciprocity also applies to antagonistic behavior.

A major benefit of revealing your interests is that you double that probability that the other party will disclose hers.

28

Negotiate issues simultaneously, not sequentially

Many people negotiate in the same way that they would run a business meeting: by strict agenda. They just list all issues under negotiation and then attempt to reach an agreement on each one, in sequence.

Try to answer this before reading further: What disadvantages might this linear approach have?

If you hypothesized that negotiators following a strict agenda are more likely to take a completely positional (demanding) approach, you're right. The key for negotiators is to handle several parts of a deal at the same time. This approach has several advantages. First, it prevents negotiators from being completely positional. Second, it forces them to prioritize their values and preferences across several issues. Third, it may spark the brilliant idea of considering distinct packages or combinations of agreement terms.

> The key for negotiators is to handle several parts of a deal at the same time.

Consider a case of two negotiators handling three issues in a sales deal: price, volume, and delivery. Ms. Buyer wants a low price, low volume, and fast delivery. Mr. Seller wants a high price, high volume, and slow delivery. On the surface, their interests seem completely opposed. In other words, it looks like a fixed-sum negotiation.

Now imagine that Ms. Buyer has carefully laid out the priority she gives each issue by splitting 100 points among them: 50 points for price, 35 for delivery, and 15 for volume (see table).

As the seller table reveals, Mr. Seller's values for the three negotiation issues are a little different: Price is still the most important issue (50 points), but volume is second (35 points) and delivery last (15 points).

We also see that Ms. Buyer ideally wants lowest price, lowest volume, and fastest delivery. If that happened, based on the table, she would get 20 + 5 + 15 = 40 points. That represents the buyer's desired objective.

BUYER	Price (50 total)	Volume (15 total)	Delivery speed (35 total)
Low (slow)	20	5	0
Med-low	15	4	2
Med	10	3	6
Med-high	5	2	12
High (fast)	0	1	15

SELLER	Price (50 total)	Volume (35 total)	Delivery speed (15 total)
Low	0	0	5
Med-low	5	2	4
Med	10	6	3
Med-high	15	12	2
High	20	15	1

Let's suppose these parties decide to negotiate each issue separately. Remember that in the real world, they wouldn't know each other's preferences. Here's how the negotiation might go:

> *Buyer*: It has been a real pleasure to learn about your product. But I have to be honest with you: We are price-restricted. We absolutely need your lowest price.
>
> *Seller*: Well, we have a great-quality, unique product. So we deserve a high price.
>
> *Buyer*: Then we might not have a deal.
>
> (One hour passes.)
>
> *Buyer*: We seem to be at two extremes on price. How about we just meet in the middle?
>
> *Seller*: I guess we can live with that.
>
> *Buyer*: Okay, then let's talk about volume. We want to minimize our commitment here, so we need only a small lot of your product.
>
> *Seller*: Unfortunately, we're designed to sell big lots. But you'll definitely love our product, so you're better off with a bigger volume, anyway.

Buyer: I'm not authorized to approve that.

Seller: Well, the price we talked about is based on a high-volume purchase.

(Another hour passes.)

Seller: There is no way I can go with that volume. I might be able to meet you in the middle, though.

Buyer: That would work.

Seller: Let's talk about delivery. We can offer our standard terms.

Buyer: No, we need this ASAP!

Seller: Sorry. Our policy clearly states that our standard delivery is several weeks.

Buyer: That just won't work. I'm being way too generous, but can we meet in the middle again?

Seller: I'll probably lose my job, but in the spirit of closing this deal…okay.

The buyer and seller would each make a total of 19 points on this deal (buyer gets sum of: medium price = 10; medium volume = 3; medium delivery = 6; and seller gets 10+6+3).

Had they negotiated the issues as a package, they might have realized that volume was relatively more important to Mr. Seller, whereas delivery speed was more important for Ms. Buyer.

That could have led to the following conversation:

Buyer: I see several moving parts to this deal: price, volume, and delivery. We care about all these issues, but price is most important. And we need to get to market fast, so we also care a lot about delivery.

Seller: We need a reasonable price, so I definitely can't concede too much on price. But my company cares a lot about volume, so we can give better prices with bigger lots. We might be able to work with you on delivery.

Buyer: Would you be willing to give me the fast delivery I need if I buy a greater volume?

TRUTH

29

Logrolling (I scratch your back, you scratch mine)

Logrolling is making mutually beneficial trade-offs between the issues on the table.

The term *logrolling* is derived from political science, where it describes how one party might support another's bill or legislation in return for reciprocal support. In that domain, logrolling has a slightly sleazy connotation. In negotiation, logrolling is smart, not sleazy.

To logroll effectively, negotiators must do the following.

- Identify more than one issue under negotiation. (Otherwise, there is no possibility for trade-offs.)
- Have different preferences concerning the issues.
- Be able to mix-and-match different alternatives for each issue.

If a negotiator is positional or demanding, logrolling will be much more difficult. Logrolling is the art and science of being firm, but flexible. A negotiator needs to be firm about the issues most important to her but flexible on things that are not as important. For example, consider Veronica, a busy executive who was "negotiating" with a childcare provider (babysitter). Hourly wage was hugely important to the babysitter, but for Vicky, having control over the provider's vacations was the most important issue. The solution? Higher pay in exchange for vacations controlled by the employer!

It's hard to imagine why negotiators fail to logroll when it would clearly be in their best interests. The key roadblock is the destructive and pervasive fixed-pie perception. Negotiators may erroneously assume that the other party's interests are directly and completely opposed to their own interests. In this sense, they falsely project their unique preferences onto the other party.

> A negotiator needs to be firm about the issues most important to her but flexible on things that are not as important.

It is far more likely that the other party will have preferences and values different from ours. This asymmetry gives negotiations much more potential for win-win outcomes.

Consider the logrolling of a buyer and seller from Truth 28.

> *Buyer*: It seems that there are three issues under consideration: price, volume, and delivery. Do you see it that way? I care about all the issues, but frankly price is most important, delivery is a close second, and I have some flexibility on volume, but only if I can get good terms on the other issues.

> *Seller*: Thanks for sharing that. My company cares about price, so we can't be too flexible there. But I'm interested in your ideas on volume and delivery. We are a volume-based seller. So, I need to be firm on volume, but I can often meet just-in-time delivery needs, provided you can meet our price and volume needs.

> *Buyer*: That gives me an idea. What's more attractive to you: medium volume and medium delivery or high volume and fast delivery? We'd rather go with high volume and fast delivery.

> *Seller*: My company is in complete agreement on that. So should we go with the highest volume and the fastest delivery?

> *Buyer*: That's what I am saying.

Secretly, you and I know that Ms. Buyer and Mr. Seller each net 16 points on this volume-delivery trade-off. Further, agreeing on a medium price would give them each 10 points. That results in 26 points for each party. This is a dramatic improvement over the 19 points they got in the no-tradeoff agreement. One of them might even get a promotion. Beyond that, both of them have gotten closer to their target and, most importantly, there is no alternate deal that is simultaneously better for both parties.

TRUTH

30

Make multiple offers of equivalent value simultaneously

One negotiation strategy that virtually guarantees that negotiators do not leave money on the table is the multiple offer strategy. How does it work? First, before beginning the negotiation, the negotiator has to unbundle the issues.

For example, consider the story of Evelyn. When seeking a job, she took the advice of a savvy employment counselor, and when her interviews led to a discussion about her salary history, she avoided the topic, saying, "Let's see if we're a good fit for each other before we talk about that issue."

The interview went well, and the decision maker was clearly interested and began the negotiation for what Evelyn's total remuneration package might be.

Obviously, salary was important to Evelyn, but given that she was a single mother, there were several other key factors: work hour flexibility, ability to do private consulting in the office space in the evenings (Evelyn is a therapist), reimbursement for clinician training and testing (to become licensed), and, of course, paid vacation days per year. Thus, Evelyn was able to identify five issues: salary, flextime, consulting privileges, licensing fee reimbursement, and vacation days.

As a second step, Evelyn knew she had to prioritize the issues. That was hard. So she pictured 100 poker chips in her mind and stacked them up in five piles to reflect how important each of the five concerns was in relation to the others. This is how she eventually stacked up the chips:

Salary (50)

Consulting privileges (20), a lucrative way to enhance her income

Flextime (15)

Licensing fee reimbursement (5)

Vacation days (10)

Evelyn was like most people: Salary was very important to her. But, as you see, other issues could make or break her quality of life. In particular, having some flexibility in her schedule and having the ability to use the office for her private consulting practice were important concerns.

After unbundling and considering the priority of the issues, the next step for Evelyn was to create three combinations of relatively equal value to her: packages A, B, and C:

Evelyn was like most people: salary was very important to her. But other issues could make or break her quality of life.

Package A: Salary of $100,000 (what the company was offering), complete flextime, three weeks paid vacation, reimbursement for licensing fees, and unlimited consulting.

Package B: Salary of $130,000, no flextime, three weeks paid vacation, no licensing fee reimbursement, and consulting opportunities under control of employer.

Package C: Salary of $120,000, three days a week of flextime, no licensing reimbursement, consulting opportunities for two days a week, and three weeks paid vacation.

Evelyn looked hard at these until she was certain she felt indifferent about which of the three packages she was offered. She was at the point where she would be willing to roll a dice and have the employer choose any of these; and she would feel equally happy.

31

Postsettlement
settlements

"Who's your favorite negotiator?" people often ask me. Many expect me to say Henry Kissinger or Donald Trump. But instead I say Professor Howard Raiffa of Harvard University. Wait, you might say, aren't professors just armchair theoreticians? Howard Raiffa is a gifted theoretician, to be sure, but he is also an amazing negotiator. So his book, *The Art and Science of Negotiation*, is chock-full of brilliant approaches to real-life negotiations.

When I first read Raiffa's description of postsettlement settlements, I was struck by its utter simplicity and elegance. Yet I haven't met a single business person who knew about it. Once they learn about it, though, they become like me: addicted.

So what is a postsettlement settlement?

Bob and Susan Sanderson are exercise nuts, but they draw the line when it comes to hauling massive specimens of new exercise equipment to their home and down the stairs to their home gym. So, when they responded to a sale at their local Costco by buying an unbelievably heavy new contraption for their home, they negotiated with Costco to have it delivered to their home. Those were the terms.

The day of the arrival came, and the driver was visibly not happy to have to heft the great and clumsy box from his truck into their house. As a matter of fact, he stated that he would only deliver to the front steps. Not *up* the steps, just *to* the steps. Ideally, the Sandersons wanted him to come through the garage and down the stairs into the basement. No doing.

The Sandersons took this as an opportunity to create a postsettlement settlement. They correctly ascertained the delivery driver's interest to be primarily financial and theirs to be primarily physical—meaning Bob did not want to have hernia operation #3. So, the Sandersons suggested that perhaps for an additional $50, the delivery driver might be willing to bring the contraption through the garage and down the stairs to the gym. They also determined that one of his concerns would be to avoid them accusing him of soiling their carpet or damaging their house. They said that they were not worried about the carpet and would take responsibility for any damage if the thing slipped. They also iced the cake by mentioning that they would pay in cash.

Thus, a postsettlement settlement represents a mutual improvement over a given deal that both parties currently find acceptable.

About 75 percent of negotiators, given an opportunity for a postsettlement settlement, are able to mutually improve upon the deal.

Think also about the motivation negotiators have when they go back to negotiate after a deal has been reached. If they think they can bully, badger, or harangue the other party into giving up more of the pie, they would be sadly mistaken. Rather, negotiators must realize that the only way to improve their own outcomes is by improving the other party's outcomes.

A postsettlement settlement represents a mutual improvement over a given deal that both parties currently find acceptable.

TRUTH

32

Contingent agreements

If logrolling are Chevys and postsettlement settlements are BMWs, then contingent agreements are Ferraris.

Sometimes negotiators vehemently disagree about a current state of affairs or what can plausibly be expected to happen in the future. Sometimes such disagreements can be resolved by consulting experts or conducting research. However, negotiators often cannot resolve such disagreements because no relevant data exists, or negotiators disagree regarding the data's relevance or interpretation. In such situations, negotiators can reach resolutions using contingent contracts.

Contingent contracts are if-then agreements that specify conditions under which specific actions will result in specific outcomes. Smart negotiators use contingent contracts in many, if not most, business negotiations. They do this because contingent contracts open up the possibility of win-win deals—they capitalize on negotiators' differing views of the world.

> Contingent contracts are if-then agreements that specify conditions under which specific actions will result in specific outcomes.

Picture this scenario. The state of California is surprised by an earthquake. Okay, it wasn't surprised, but it hadn't planned on one right then. The Nimitz Bridge has collapsed, preventing the crossing of San Francisco Bay. Bridges are out and lanes knocked akimbo across that part of the state, not to mention sewage and drainage pipes being misaligned. The state needs help, and fast. It will get some Federal money, but aside from a maze of makeshift detours, some hundreds of thousands of workers cannot commute to work. So, what does the state do? Like any government bureaucracy, the state shifts into high gear and puts out a call for bids to repair damages. This could take forever. Right?

However, what the state does that is different, and pretty sharp, is that once the lowest bid is landed—and I won't go into how the system we favor means most things we drive on are built by the lowest bidder—it negotiates a delivery. It knew money was important to the contractors and that time was important to the state's getting back to normal.

The contractor knew the reality of how long it takes to build or repair roads on this scale. But it also had an eye on its bottom line. Show me the money!

So the state negotiated a contingency contract for the delivery of the sum of all repairs needed. It set an aggressive deadline: six months. If the contractor delivered all the repairs on time, it would get a multimillion dollar bonus. This put both negotiators on the same side of the table. The state wanted the repairs done now, and the contractor wanted as much money as could be had.

What they eventually landed on was an agreement with the stated bonus, but also penalties if the contractor went over the agreed-upon deadline. The contractor was willing to shoulder the risk of making less money in the face of the opportunity to make much more. And, don't you know, all those repairs were made on time, well within the deadline. The contractor got its bonus, and traffic was back to normal in the state of California.

Think about a negotiation in which your view of the world was misaligned with the other party's. Could you have crafted a contingent agreement?

Think now about a time when you had a different risk attitude than your counterparty did. Perhaps you were risk averse and the counterparty was risk tolerant. Might you have crafted a contingent arrangement based on this mismatch? There was one instance in which my husband and I disagreed about whether I would be able to drive back to our house from an appointment in time for him to drive my car to an important event. (For various reasons, we both wanted to use my car.) Because he was much more risk averse than I was in this case, I told him that if I failed to return by a certain time, I would buy and prepare all the food for the dinner party we were hosting the next week, a task we normally would have shared. He took me up on the proposal (which, by the way, I lost).

Another case in which contingent agreements may be used is when negotiators have different time preferences. Some people want immediate payoffs; the counterparty might be more interested in long-term payoffs.

To be effective, contingent agreements should meet three criteria, at minimum: incentive alignment, enforceability, and measurability. First and foremost, continent contracts should not give negotiators an incentive to work at cross-purposes to each other. Rather, contingent contracts should align objectives, as in the case of the California road repair construction. Second, I strongly encourage negotiators to formalize contingent contracts in writing, with appropriate legal counsel. Finally, but still important, decide in advance how the terms of the agreement will be measured.

To be effective, contingent agreements should meet three criteria, at minimum: incentive alignment, enforceability, and measurability.

33

Are you an enlightened negotiator?

Imagine you're negotiating with your identical twin, a person with a similar personality to yours. How would the negotiation turn out? Lovefest? Catfight? Standoff? If the answer is anything except a win-win lovefest, we've got a problem, Houston. One of you needs to change.

Suppose you're negotiating with a counterparty whom you trust and admire and wish to have a long-term relationship with. How big do you want the pie to be? This is not a trick question. How do you want to slice that large pie? This is a trickier question. You might say, "Down the middle." Or, "Fairly."

Okay, let's change the question. Suppose you're about to negotiate with someone you don't trust, don't like, don't respect. How big do you want the total pie to be? If you said, "As big as possible," you're right. Now, how do you want to slice this pie? Hopefully, you want to drive the counterparty down to her barely acceptable set of terms to keep all the added value for yourself.

These two extreme cases reveal an important point: Whether we love or hate the other party, trust or distrust her, will ever see her again or not, we always want to extract the maximum potential value of a deal. But we may have different reasons for wanting this. In the first case (when I adore you), I want to divide a large pie between us because I value my own welfare and yours. In the second case, the only reason I want a big pie of resources to divide is that I want to grab every dime for myself, and I know that there will be more for me if I can discover it.

> Whether we love or hate the other party, trust or distrust her, will ever see her again or not, we always want to extract the maximum potential value of a deal.

Thus, one of the key revelations related to win-win negotiations is that we should always want to maximize the pie, regardless of circumstance or whether we are altruists or opportunists. Win-win negotiation can be used solely for self-interest, but it is also the best strategy in completely altruistic negotiations.

Win-win negotiation can be used solely for self-interest, but it is also the best strategy in completely altruistic negotiations.

It would be naïve to believe that the counterparties you encounter in life are not just as smart and motivated as you are. The enlightened negotiator embraces the fact that the counterparty is smart, ambitious, and has complex, multifaceted motivations.

One of my earliest experiences with enlightened negotiations came at a large pharmaceutical company engaged in a multiday negotiation training program. "We've invited key clients to this training," the pharmaceutical folks who had developed the program told me. I was aghast—they had invited the "enemy" to hear all their negotiation secrets! They went on to explain that they strongly preferred that the people with whom they negotiate daily be just as expert as they were in the skill of deriving mutual gains through win-win agreements. This was a revelation for me. One of the worst fates that can befall you as a negotiator is to have to reach an agreement with someone who knows a lot less about negotiation than you do. The unenlightened negotiator often hasn't unbundled the negotiation or prioritized—or even considered—his interests; thus, he clings to positions and demands as if they were rafts in a stormy ocean.

The enlightened negotiator, on the other hand, realizes that the best counterparty would in fact be her identical twin—someone who is every bit as knowledgeable, smart, and motivated as she is.

TRUTH

34

The reciprocity principle

Shortly after the United States entered World War II, the Americans joined the British in launching costly bombing raids over Germany. Part of the intent was to demoralize the Germans and break their will. The U.S. and UK believed that a series of steady bombing raids would demoralize the Germans and cause them to retreat. However, the plan to demoralize did not work. Research reports conducted by the Office of Strategic Services that compared heavily and lightly bombed areas did not find significant differences in civilians' will to resist.

Several other conflicts follow the same psychological pattern, such as Pearl Harbor, South Africa, and North Vietnam. In all of these instances, the aggressor works under the faulty belief that aggression will lead to submission in the target. However, inevitably, aggression invites aggression.

The *reciprocity principle* is probably the most important but least understood concept in psychology. It characterizes relationships among people, groups, and warring nations. The reciprocity principle is quite simply the tendency for people to treat others the way they are treated.

Salespeople understand the reciprocity effect. Excellent salespeople know that small acts of generosity create powerful psychological obligations that result in big sales. Real estate agents also understand the reciprocity effect (which is why they give you calendars and refrigerator magnets). The reciprocity effect does not know cultural boundaries, as it has been documented in nearly every country in the world. And feelings of indebtedness to others run deep; if one group receives a favor from another group but is unable to return the favor immediately, it carries that debt into the next generation to repay.

> The reciprocity principle is quite simply the tendency for people to treat others the way they are treated.

Assume that the counterparty is every bit as smart and motivated as you are.

Why, then, do so many well-meaning negotiators behave like bulldogs in negotiation and wonder why the other party chooses to escalate instead of back down? The answer, I think, is simple: We hold a psychological double standard when it comes to using force. We think that if we use force, we can intimidate and weaken the other party. Yet we believe that if someone uses force with us, we will retaliate. Again, the model of the fraternal twin is key here: Assume that the counterparty is every bit as smart and motivated as you are.

So, when you think about flexing muscle in a negotiation, be warned that doing so will most definitely increase the probability that the counterparty will flex his muscle, too.

If the reciprocity principle characterizes the use of aggression and competition in negotiation, it certainly applies to the cooperative, constructive aspect of negotiation. In other words, if I use a trusting, relationship-building strategy in negotiation, have I increased or decreased the probability that you will respond in a constructive, trusting fashion? Answer: I have increased it.

.

TRUTH

35

The reinforcement
principle

A group of sneaky students got together before class and decided to test the power of the reinforcement principle. Whenever the instructor walked on the right side of the classroom, they attentively smiled, nodded, and sat forward in their seats. However, when the instructor paced over to the left side of the classroom, the students slumped, averted their eyes, and disengaged. On which side of the classroom did the teacher spend the most time, the right or the left? The obvious answer is that he spent dramatically more time on the right side of the classroom. The students had positively reinforced the speaker's behavior. Yet, the instructor was unaware of why he ended up on the right side of the room by the end of the lecture. Which brings up an important point about reinforcement: It occurs at a level below our threshold of awareness.

Under what conditions would you want to use reinforcement in negotiation? Answer: Anytime you want to increase a certain behavior. In negotiation, people emit various behaviors, some pleasant and constructive—and some offensive and destructive. Ideally, we want to encourage the counterparty to emit behaviors that will help us expand the pie. We can do this if we follow certain principles of behavioral reinforcement.

As simple as this psychology sounds, it is easy to screw it up. The main things to remember about reinforcement are these.

Under what conditions would you want to use reinforcement in negotiation? Answer: Anytime you want to increase a certain behavior.

- **Be immediate**—We're talking about seconds when it comes to rewarding behavior. So, if you wait several minutes to nod and smile to the counterparty, your have missed your window to reward her behavior.

- **Be unambiguous**—Your reward should be clear and simple, such as a clear and simple nod, an open smile, eye contact, or a heartfelt compliment.

- **Reward behaviors, not underlying states**—The reinforcement principle works great when it comes to behaviors. Don't get caught up in trying to reward an attitude, disposition, or intention of the other party. My rule of thumb is to stick to whatever behaviors can be pointed to. For example, don't try to reinforce someone for speaking truthfully. However, reward someone for opening up his binder or sharing a company report.

- **Be consistent**—If you sometimes reward a given behavior and sometimes fail to acknowledge or even perhaps punish that same behavior, you send a mixed message to the other party. Be consistent in your rewards.

All of the following actions may be considered rewards in most contexts. They build a cooperative foundation and do not require us to give up any of the previous zone of possible agreement (ZOPA):

- Smiling
- Nodding
- Maintaining eye contact (in many cultures, but eye contact in some cultures can be threatening and a sign of dominance, not liking)
- Verbal phrases, such as, "I like that."
- Or, "I appreciate that."
- Or, "That is great."
- Or even, "Tell me more."

TRUTH

36

The similarity principle

Think about the last cocktail party you attended where you met someone for the first time. Chances are, you spent the first part of your conversation trying to establish a point of similarity. When people meet for the first time, they relentlessly search for a point of similarity. For example, "Do I detect a Texas accent?"; "Have you ever met my friend, Rhonda?"; "Where did you go to school?"

The irrepressible urge to find a point of similarity in others is hardwired in most of us. It is our primitive way of sizing up whether someone is friend or foe, threat or opportunity. Someone who is like us might share some of our gene pool and work with us, not against us.

Negotiators do the same thing. They try to find a point of similarity. And, indeed, the similarity game is often part of the negotiation pregame.

> The irrepressible urge to find a point of similarity in others is hardwired in most of us.

Evidence for the similarity principle is overwhelming. In one investigation, people were randomly divided into two groups: dot overestimators and dot underestimators. (Everyone had to guess how many dots were on a page.)[17] Then people were informed they were either a dot overestimator or a dot underestimator. (Of course, they were actually told at random if they were a dot overestimator or a dot underestimator.) Next, they engaged in negotiation with someone who was either described as a dot underestimator or a dot overestimator. The results were dramatic: People behaved much more cooperatively with people who were part of the same dot estimator group. This was shocking because who in the heck cares about dots anyway? The point, however, is worth noting: People cooperate more with others who are supposedly similar to them and compete more with others who are different from them. It certainly behooves all of us to find a point of similarity with the counterparty.

In another investigation, marchers in a political demonstration were more likely to sign a petition if the requester was dressed like them.[18] Moreover, they signed the petition without even reading it when the requester was dressed similarly to them!

It certainly behooves all of us to find a point of similarity with the counterparty.

The similarity principle works also for social networks. If you can find a common point of connection that is a similar person, this creates a psychological obligation to like the other person. Suppose, for example, that Mary is negotiating with Ned. They have never met, but Mary learns that Ned knows (and likes) Jose. Mary also likes Jose. This means that Mary and Ned are most likely going to want to get along, to put the entire social network in a state of harmony.

37

Know when to drop an anchor

In one investigation, people were asked to guess how many African countries were in the United Nations.[19] Most people don't know the answer to this question without a Google search, so they guess. In this particular study, people were standing in front of a wheel of fortune. Half of the time, the researcher spun the wheel of fortune and it landed on a high number (such as 100); the other half of the time, the number was much lower (such as 10). How did the random wheel-of-fortune number affect people's judgments about the number of African countries in the United Nations? Even though it is illogical for a random number to have anything to do with making this guess, it strongly affected people's judgments. The people who saw the high number adjusted their guess downward, but not downward enough. (The average guess was 50.) The people who saw the low number adjusted their guess upward, but not upward enough. (The average guess was 15.) The actual number of African countries in the United Nations is 53.[20]

What is interesting about the wheel-of-fortune study is that everybody knows that wheels of fortune are based on chance. Thus, in some sense, people should have completely discounted the number that was displayed on the wheel of fortune. This brings up another important point about the anchoring effect: Even when the initial anchor is obviously arbitrary or downright silly, it still exerts a powerful impact on people's judgments.

The *anchoring effect* refers to the fact that people tend to make judgments based upon an initial starting point and then adjust upward or downward, but they fail to make sufficiently large adjustments.

Another example: People were asked to guess how many physicians were listed in the Manhattan phone book. Certainly, no one knows that information off the top of her head. Some people

People tend to make judgments based upon an initial starting point and then adjust upward or downward, but they fail to make sufficiently large adjustments.

were first asked whether the number was greater than or less than 100. Other people were first asked whether the number was greater than or less than 1,000,000. Obviously, there are more than 100 doctors in Manhattan, but certainly less than a million. However, these two different anchors caused people to make very different guestimates about the actual number of physicians in Manhattan.

In negotiation, your opening offer acts as an anchor—so does the counterparty's opening offer. If you are a buyer, your low initial bid might be unacceptable to the seller but will act as an anchor, nevertheless.

Anchors can be numbers, but they can also be your supporting arguments and data. Anchors have more staying power when they are supplemented with facts, data, and logic. Thus, it is much more powerful to justify your opening offer with relevant information and facts than to simply state the offer.

> Anchors have more staying power when they are supplemented with facts, data, and logic.

TRUTH

38

The framing effect

Which would you rather have?

A. $10,000 for sure

or

B. A 50-50 chance of winning $20,000 or nothing

This tantalizing proposition is an approach-approach conflict because both options are pretty attractive. (We'd like both of them!) However, we have a little bit of an internal conflict in choosing because as much as we would like to get $20,000, there is a 50 percent chance that we would walk away with nothing. When most people are given the A or B choice, the large majority choose A. (About 85 percent of the students in my MBA and executive courses would rather have $10,000 for sure than a 50-50 chance of winning twice as much money.)

This phenomenon illustrates a basic tenet of human behavior, called *risk aversion.* When it comes to choosing among attractive courses of action, most people would rather have a bird in the hand than go beating around the bush.

However, let's turn the tables around. Imagine that someone has you at gunpoint in a dark alley, late at night, and offers you the following choice:

C. Lose $10,000

Or

D. Submit to a 50-50 chance of losing $20,000 or nothing?

(To make this seem more real, imagine that this person has the ability to extract this money from you.)

> When it comes to choosing among attractive courses of action, most people would rather have a bird in the hand than go beating around the bush.

This is an avoidance-avoidance conflict because neither option is attractive. In fact, both options suck. However, you are being held at gunpoint, and you have to choose. The majority of people in this situation choose the gamble—in other words, they opt to flip the coin and take a risk that they might lose a huge sum of money, but they might not end up losing anything. This behavior illustrates a basic tenet of human behavior, called *risk-seeking behavior*.

But now, we have a conundrum: How can people be both risk averse and risk seeking?

This is where Nobel prize-winning psychologist Daniel Kahneman of Princeton University comes to the rescue. According to Amos Tversky and Daniel Kahneman, whether people avoid or embrace risk depends upon how the problem or decision is *framed*.[21] When people are asked to make approach-approach decisions (that is, choosing a sure good thing or a gamble that might lead to something much more attractive), most people are risk averse. However, if that same problem is framed as an avoidance-avoidance problem, the tables turn and people are much more likely to gamble!

Indeed, almost any decision in our lives can be framed as a gain or a loss relative to *something*. Quite frankly, our point of reference for defining gains and losses is pretty arbitrary. A reference point defines what a person considers to be a gain or a loss. Savvy negotiators know how to frame the offers they make to the other party by carefully selecting points of reference.

Max Bazerman, Tom Magliozzi, and Margaret Neale demonstrated the powerful framing effecting negotiation. They told some negotiators that they should try to "cut their losses"; other negotiators were told that they were trying to "maximize their gains."[22] However, in both cases, their objective financial situations were completely identical. In other words, the only difference was how the negotiators framed their own financial situation.

> Indeed, almost any decision in our lives can be framed as a gain or a loss relative to *something*.

Bazerman, Magliozzi, and Neale expected that the negotiators who were told to cut their losses would behave a lot like the person confronted in the dark alley: In other words, they would behave in a much more risk-seeking fashion. That is what happened: Negotiators who were put the mindset of cutting their losses made fewer concessions in the negotiation and reached more impasses than did negotiators who were told to maximize their gains. In short, these negotiators took a gamble by refusing all offers in hand and decided on a risky course of action that involved walking away from a sure deal (in hopes of a better deal!).

This effect clearly shows that negotiators who have the mindset of minimizing their losses adopt more risky bargaining strategies, preferring to hold out for a better but more risky settlement. In contrast, negotiators who are told to maximize their gains are more likely to take the bird in the hand.

Obviously, it is in your best interest to put your opponent in a "gain" frame. This will increase the chance that the opponent will take your offer. If the counterparty views your proposal as a loss, he will do something risky, like stalking out of the room.

The framing effect is a powerful, two-edged sword: You can frame others, but you can also be framed! So, before any negotiation, think about your reference points!

TRUTH

39

Responding to tempertantrums

Several negotiators, such as Donald Trump, are renowned for throwing temper tantrums at the bargaining table. Often this means throwing plateware, stalking out, making threats, and using verbal abuse. Is this behavior effective in eliciting concessions from the counterparty?

Many temper tantrums are not genuine. Rather, they are carefully orchestrated displays of emotion designed to evoke a response in the counterparty. This is the difference between felt emotion and strategic displays of emotion.

In a staged study situation[23] to determine whether it is a good or bad idea to display negative emotion at the bargaining table, negotiators were given a "deteriorating best alternative to a negotiated agreement (BATNA)," meaning that their alternative courses of action were disappearing fast, and the only game that was left in town

> Many temper tantrums are... carefully orchestrated displays of emotion designed to evoke a response in the counterparty.

was to work with negotiator X. Negotiator X was coached to adopt one of three emotional styles: very cordial and considerate (Ms. Nice); extremely rude and demanding (Ms. Temper); or neither rude nor nice (Ms. Neutral).

All the negotiators were then put in a take-it-or-leave-it situation by negotiator X. The question was which of the three emotional styles would be most effective. It turns out that Ms. Temper was the least effective. Perhaps out of spite or perhaps because they were so angry, no one wanted to give business to Ms. Temper, even when their BATNAs were rapidly deteriorating.

In another investigation, a negotiator made a take-it-or-leave-it offer and in some conditions, made a joke (for example, "I will throw in my pet frog"); the other half of the time, the negotiator did not make a joke. In both situations, the contents of the offer were the same. However, acceptance rates were not the same. People liked the negotiator with the sense of humor more than the humorless negotiator.[24]

40

What's your sign? (Know your disputing style)

Which of the following phrases have you used or heard used in a negotiation? Be honest. Better yet, ask your colleagues to fill this out for you. Give yourself 1 point if you have ever said this phrase and 2 points if you say something like it often. If that phrase is not in your vocabulary, give yourself a 0.

1. ____ That's not the way we do things here.
2. ____ That is my final offer.
3. ____ You will have to do better than that; otherwise, we don't have a deal.
4. ____ What is your most important issue?
5. ____ According to my records, that is not what we agreed to.
6. ____ I want to share some of my interests with you.
7. ____ I am calling my attorney (or any mention of an attorney).
8. ____ That is the most ridiculous thing I have ever heard.
9. ____ I would like to understand more about your key value drivers.

First add up your Power score (items #2, #3, #8). Then, add up your Rights score (items #1, #5, #7). Finally, add up your Interests score (items #4, #6, #9).

* * *

Jeanne Brett spent several years in coal mines watching extremely contentious negotiations between labor and management unfold. She did the same thing at airline negotiations with union reps and management. In her book, *Getting Disputes Resolved* (with coauthors Steve Goldberg and William Ury), she discovered that nearly everything that people said could be chunked into one of three major buckets: interests, rights, or power. Accordingly, Brett and Goldberg developed their theory of disputing styles called the Interests, Rights, and Power Model.[25]

■ **Power**—Power moves are any statements that attempt to force another person to do something he would otherwise not do. Parents do this with children, and people of different status levels do this a lot. For example, "If you don't do X, I will terminate you." Power moves also include one-upsmanship or hurling insults.

Threats to withdraw your business are power moves. For example, one sister might say "If you don't give the orange to me, I am going to tell mom that you drove her car without asking."

- **Rights**—Rights moves are those that reference standards, norms, customs, rules, guidelines, legal rights, or precedents. Statements such as, "This is not the way we do things" or excessive focus on bureaucracy are examples of rights-based moves. The rights-based negotiator attempts to invoke precedents. The rights-based sister might say, "I sent you an email dated February 22, 2007 in which I claimed that orange."

- **Interests**—Interest-based negotiators attempt to get past the demands that the parties might have and focus on the underlying goals and interests. The interests-based sister might say, "What are your most pressing interests regarding the orange? For me personally, I need to get my scone business going, so having that zest is imperative."

If your P score was highest, you tend to use power moves in your negotiations. If your R score was highest, you use rights-based moves. If your I score was highest, congratulations—you use interest-based negotiation.

Once you know the I-R-P model, it is impossible not to spontaneously categorize people. For example, the other day, I witnessed a blue car make a sharp left-hand turn to grab a coveted parking spot. The blue car pulled quickly in front of a white car that was poised to turn right into the same coveted space. The driver of the white car immediately shot the finger (power move). The driver of the blue car explained that he indeed had his blinker on before the other car did and therefore was entitled to the space (rights-based move).

The same thing happens in airports. Think about the last time you were at the ticket counter and an angry customer demanded a ticket change. The gate agent refuses. The angry customer demands to see her boss (power move). The ticket agent recites rules printed on the back of the ticket (rights move). The even angrier customer says, "Hey, I can read. I went to school" (power move). The ticket agent then says, "Sir, you will have to leave; I have to serve other customers" (rights move). Finally, the superior emerges and says,

Negotiations need to be trilingual. You need to be able to use interest, rights, and power at the appropriate time.

"What is the problem here? Let's take a look at what we can do" (interests-based move).

The point here is not that you need to always use interest phrases and extinguish rights and power move ones from your vocabulary. Negotiations need to be trilingual. You need to be able to use interest, rights, and power at the appropriate time.

TRUTH

41

Using power responsibly

Beer ads advise that people should drink responsibly. The same advice is true in negotiation: Use power responsibly. Power is the use of force or coercion—psychological, behavioral, or physical.

- You use *psychological* power when you threaten to "never trust someone again."

- You use *behavioral* power when you threaten to "take all the money out of the joint checking account."

- You use *physical* power when you hit the other party in the gut.

First and foremost, I don't advocate using physical power under any circumstance, except possibly self-defense. However, there are times in life when you might be justified in using psychological or behavioral power.

The main motive for using power is to move the party off an unreasonable position or stance. For example, if you have exhausted your time to spend negotiating a deal, you might decide to get up, start packing your briefcase and say, "This is my final offer." That would be a power move, and you would use it after you had exhausted all other strategies in the time that you had to negotiate.

> The main motive for using power is to move the party off an unreasonable position or stance.

The second thing to keep in mind is that when you use power, you have statistically doubled the probability that the other party will use power with you. So, you need to be serious about using power. And, you need to know how to get Genie back in the bottle.

The final thing to keep in mind is that people often feel embarrassed succumbing to the other party because they want to preserve their dignity. To compensate, you need to engage in a variety of face-saving behaviors.

TRUTH

42

Saving face

According to negotiation expert Morton Deutsch, saving face is a negotiator's most sacred possession. Face is the value we put on our public image, reputation, and status in negotiations.

Part of using power responsibly is creating a way that both parties can come back to the negotiation table without fear of social censure or loss of self-esteem.

Negotiators often get so caught up in who's right and who's wrong determinations that they make it virtually impossible for people to return to the table with their dignity in hand.

> Face is the value we put on our public image, reputation, and status in negotiations.

Moreover, people in the United States often do not appreciate how important face-saving concerns are for members of different cultures. For example, if I have just embarrassed you in front of your boss, I have put you in an awkward position.

Saving face works in two ways: helping others protect and maintain their dignity, and managing your own esteem needs.

All of us care about how other people see us, and we have our own need for self-respect. However, the following situations will heighten people's need to save face:

- When negotiations are conducted in a public setting
- When people are accountable to a group or a superior
- When people negotiate in teams (as opposed to negotiating as individuals)
- When there are status differences between negotiators
- When negotiators have naturally thin skin

You can measure negotiators' face-saving needs by using a scale, called the Face Threat Sensitivity (FTS) scale. (If you want to see how thin your own skin is according to the FTS scale items: 1. I don't respond well to direct criticism, 2. My feelings get hurt easily, 3. I am pretty thin-skinned, see the article "Face threat sensitivity in negotiation: Roadblock to agreement and joint gain." [26])People with high FTS have a lower threshold for detecting and responding to threats to their face (dignity). In other words, it does not take much to get them hot and bothered. Conversely, people with a low FTS have thicker skin; they don't see situations as making them look foolish, and they are not easily threatened.

In buyer-seller negotiations, fewer win-win agreements are reached when the seller has thin skin (high FTS). Moreover, in employment negotiations, job candidates with high FTS (thin skin) are less likely to make win-win deals.

Here are some of my favorite face-saving strategies to use if you sense that the other party has thin skin (and therefore, a need to save face).

> In buyer-seller negotiations, fewer win-win agreements are reached when the seller has thin skin.

- Apologize for something. ("I don't like some of the things that came out of my mouth in our discussion today. I hope you can forgive me.")

- Compliment the person. ("I think your ideas about the pricing program are particularly ingenious and refreshing.")

- Say you care about the relationship. ("I know we are focusing on the business at hand, but I want to stop for one minute and do a relationship check and reiterate how important the relationship with you is to our company.")

- Talk about how you have learned important things as a result of this process.

- Ask for feedback about how things are going on the relationship ledger. ("Look, Steve, I am new in my role here, and I would love some of your feedback at this point in the process.")

- Point out the concessions you made. ("I am conceding to you on point X.")

- Focus on the future, not the past. (People are often preoccupied with justifying their past behavior.) One my favorite lines from Ury, Brett, and Goldberg is, "We are not going to agree about the past, but we might agree about the future."

- If the other party says, "This is my final offer," don't respond with, "I don't believe you!" Instead, respond by saying, "I hear you, and I would like to respond to some particular points."

43

How to negotiate with someone you hate

So, you've got to negotiate with this person. Now what?

You will almost certainly have to negotiate with some people who have pathological personalities. You need to figure out a way to deal with the mental cases you have to negotiate with. Medicating the other person is not an option, so what can you do?

There are three important things to keep in mind when it comes to dealing with difficult people at the negotiation table.

- Replace "D" (dispositional) statements with "B" (behavioral) statements.

- Label your feelings, not people.

- Change your behaviors, not your feelings.

Let's take each of these points in turn, because if you become consumed by feelings of hate and repulsion for the other party, you are not going to be able to negotiate effectively.

Replace D statements with B statements

Consider the following statements, actually made by negotiators.

"Jack is impossible to deal with."

"Larry is always a jerk when we sit down for budget meeting."

"My supplier, Elizabeth, is psychotic in sales negotiations."

These are all examples of type D statements because they focus on the counterparty's *dispositions*. Type D statements (or "Dispositional" statements) are characterized by the belief that a given person behaves the way she does because of her personality or disposition. Dead giveaways for a type D statement are the words, "always" (for example, "Elizabeth *always* does such and such"; "Jack is *always* this way.") Type D statements locate the root of the cause of a person's behavior to that person's fundamental disposition rather than as a reaction to a situation he might be in. Type D statements are character assassinations.

If you become consumed by feelings of hate and repulsion for the other party, you are not going to be able to negotiate effectively. a

What is the solution? Replace type D (disposition) statements with type B (behavior) statements. All of the following are type B statements:

> "I hate the fact that Jack is consistently late to meetings."
>
> "I don't like the way Larry treats the junior people on the team."
>
> "I resent it when Elizabeth changes her mind after committing to a deal."

Parents often fall into the trap of making type D statements with their kids: "You are annoying"; "You are driving me crazy"; or the worst, "You are bad." The parent should rephrase these statements:

> "The way you are playing that music is annoying me."
>
> "Being asked the same question by you for the past 30 minutes makes me feel short-tempered."
>
> "Breaking DVD disks is very bad."

Label your feelings, not people

When you make statements like, "You are acting crazy," "She is aggressive," or "She is making me lose my temper," you are relinquishing all responsibility to the other party for your behavior.

Take more ownership for your negative relationships by taking more responsibility for your own feelings. Even if you can't change your feelings, you can take more responsibility. Consider the table that follows. On the left side are common statements people make in the heat of argument. On the right side are reformulations in which negotiators take more personal responsibility.

Typical statements made that do not take personal responsibility	Reformulations of these statements that reflect ownership and responsibility
"You are making me mad."	"I am feeling short-tempered."
"She is too aggressive."	"I feel resentful when I am given ultimatums."
"You are screwing up the deal."	"I feel that it is unwise for me to make a deal."
"Your offer is ridiculous."	"I am disappointed with the progress we are making."

Change your behavior, not your feelings

You most likely have a few "complex relationships" in your negotiation life—relationships that are necessary for you to engage in to conduct business, but relationships that cause you anxiety for a variety of reasons. You may have tried unsuccessfully to change your feelings about the counterparty—perhaps engaged in endless amounts of self-talk, personal pledges to try to change your feelings about a person. Yet, nothing works. You still harbor resentment toward this person.

It is perfectly okay to have venomous feelings for another person. Don't try to change those feelings at least right now. Instead, commit to changing your behavior. Be proactive. Think of three acts of cooperation you are going to commit to with the "complex relationship" in the next 10 days. Here are some steps you can take to get rolling:

- Stop by this person's office and bring her a latte.
- Send this person's subordinate a nice email complimenting her on a job well done.
- If appropriate, give this person's superior a compliment about her.
- Invite this person to lunch without business intent.
- Send this person a book or DVD that you know would be welcome.

You can even take responsibility one step further: The next time you are interacting with Ms. Complex Relationship, raise the issue of how you would like to improve your working relationship. Ask if she might share the same goal. Most often, the other person sees you as the complex relationship. Suggest some ideas. Ask for feedback. Shake hands.

TRUTH

44

How to negotiate with someone you love

Negotiating with someone you love, deeply respect, or have had a long-term relationship with is not always the walk in the park you might think it should be. Husbands and wives and dating couples are more likely to satisfice (compromise badly) and reach lose-lose outcomes!

When we think about negotiations with people that we love, there is a past, a present, and a future. When there is a lot at stake, emotions can run high. So it is best if you have a working approach.

Most of the negotiations we do in our personal lives with people that we love arise when we experience conflict. *Conflict* occurs when people perceive themselves to have incompatible interests involving scarce resources (who gets the family car for the evening), goals (where to go on a family vacation), or procedures (how to discipline children).

Many of the business negotiations we've discussed in this book have focused on purely transactional (buyer-seller) relationships. The parties in those situations sought one another out because they saw an opportunity to make a trade. For example, a seller and buyer might see a mutual opportunity. Opportunity moves people to negotiate. However, people in long-term relationships are not brought together by business opportunity; instead, they step on each other's toes and need to resolve conflict.

When it comes to conflict in personal relationships, your own view of what is going on in the relationship may not be at all what your partner thinks. Sometimes, conflict may not exist, but people feel that it does; other times, people are not aware that they have a conflict. Consider this table:

	Actual conflict	**No actual conflict**
Perceived conflict	Real conflict	False conflict
No perceived conflict	Latent conflict	Harmony

Note that when conflict actually exists and people perceive it, that is *real* conflict. When there is no actual conflict but people believe there is, that is a case of *false* conflict. Conversely, when conflict exists but people fail to perceive it, that is *latent* conflict.

Harmony speaks for itself!

Once you determine if conflict is real, you need to decide what your reaction is going to be to it. According to psychologist Carol Rusbult, there are four possible reactions: exit, loyalty, neglect, and voice.[27]

Exit occurs when one person leaves the relationship to seek greener pastures. When you exit a relationship, you actively exercise your best alternative to a negotiated agreement (BATNA).

Loyalty means you stay with your partner and just tolerate him. It means that you accept his terms and capitulate. You might simply accept the first thing he suggests and never assert your own aspirations. People are often afraid that they will hurt or insult the other party, so they capitulate to the other party. We are often uncomfortable negotiating with people we love. This, of course, is the ultimate form of satisficing. People satisfice in personal relationships because they put a greater value or utility on resolving conflict than they do on the actual outcomes involved. When people do this over time, they may rationalize, or they may become resentful.

Neglect is a passive strategy for dealing with conflict. It occurs when parties are in a standoff or impasse. Neither is engaging in a real discussion, and neither is seeking greener pastures. Unfortunately, this holding pattern will certainly cause the relationship to deteriorate.

Voice occurs when people proactively decide to try to talk about the conflict and make things better. Voice is an active strategy. It quite literally means that both parties articulate their concerns and views on the conflict. When it comes to voice, don't underestimate the power of letting people vent and express themselves. Here are some of my favorite lines for initiating a proactive discussion.

> When conflict actually exists and people perceive it, that is real conflict. When there is no actual conflict but people believe there is, that is a case of false conflict. When conflict exists but people fail to perceive it, that is latent conflict.

- I need to talk to you about something that is bothering me. I want to try to work things out before I start feeling resentful.

- I feel uncomfortable talking about our finances (car, travel schedules, household chores), but I am unhappy with our current situation and suspect you feel the same.

- Given that there has been a recent change in our finances (travel schedules, work commitments, and so on), this has led to some unanticipated and undesirable effects on me. I have some ideas to talk to you about how to make it better.

TRUTH

45

Building the winning negotiation team

Are you more effective negotiating in a team or as an individual?

Teams more often promote the win-win process because they ask relevant questions and formulate more accurate judgments about the counterparty's interests.[28] Conversely, one-on-one negotiators ask remarkably fewer questions and are more likely to harbor the fixed-pie assumption than the enlightened assumption that parties' interest may be more complementary than conflicting.

In the business world, negotiators often have some choice about who is on a team, so you should be thoughtful about whom you select. The most common team mistakes are these.

- Making the team too big. (Yes, teams can be too big.)
- Making the team too homogeneous. (Everyone is a carbon copy of everyone else.)
- The team acting as individual silos (each with her own pet agenda items rather than collaborating to present a united front).
- Lack of discipline in terms of the process that will be followed or the roles that people will take.

Here's advice on how to optimally build and prepare a team.[29]

- First and foremost, select people who are triathletes in terms of having negotiation expertise, technical expertise, and interpersonal skills. (It would scare the daylights out of me to have a team member who did not know what a BATNA was!) It is imperative to have team members with depth of expertise in the subject matter at hand. And interpersonal skills are important, as one loose cannon can bring down the whole ship.
- Be lean. Only recruit enough members to cover these three areas of skill. Teams should be ideally be 3–6 people—never double-digits.
- Prepare together as a team using common-language worksheets. If everybody on the team has his own name for the issues and his own lingo for the alternatives, it will be impossible to have discussions.

Select people who are triathletes in terms of having negotiation expertise, technical expertise, and interpersonal skills.

- Assign meaningful roles. There should be a lead spokesperson. Someone should take charge of building and running dynamic spreadsheets on which offers and counteroffers can be quickly calculated.

- The team should be in agreement about key values, such as their BATNA, their reservation point, their aspiration point, and so on.

- The team should decide what information should be revealed and what information shouldn't.

TRUTH

46

What if they arrive with a team?

If the counterparty has a team and you are negotiating solo, you should be wary about claiming and how the pie will be sliced. When a team negotiates against a lone negotiator, the lone negotiator claims about one-third less than what the team is able to claim.

By all means, you should bring a team to the table if you know in advance that the counterparty will be appearing in the form of a team.

Most negotiators are instinctively aware of the team advantage. One young manager about to embark on a business trip grabbed a professional-looking middle-aged gentleman at the last minute and told him, "Just sit in a chair and look smart." The distinguished gentleman was what the young manager called "his gray-haired equity."

If you don't have time to troll for distinguished looking middle-aged people to accompany you on business trips, I encourage you to do the next-best thing: Create a team in your own mind. I call this the *phantom team member*. Married people do this spontaneously when they make reference to having to get the approval of the other spouse, even when they don't really plan to consult the spouse. Even single people tell salespeople that they "have to talk to my wife" (when in fact, they are not married). I have a friend who wears a fake wedding ring when she buys a car.

> When a team negotiates against a lone negotiator, the lone negotiator claims about one-third less than what the team is able to claim.

It is ironic but true that when we claim not to have full authority in a bargaining situation, we gain power. This phenomenon has not been lost on psychologists, who call this factor the my *hands are tied* strategy. When we tell the counterparty that our hands are tied, we buy ourselves more time to reflect and create pressure in the counterparty to offer us better terms. This is precisely why car dealers say that they cannot offer a price reduction without consulting their manager or owner.

You will realize that you negotiate more effectively when you negotiate on behalf of someone else. Again, this is traceable to the *accountability pressure factor*, which is the tendency for people to be more assertive when they believe that someone else is watching.

If you've got the time and energy, offer to negotiate on behalf of someone else. For example, perhaps a friend is trying to return a used or opened item to a department store. Or a colleague is attempting to get an upgrade at a hotel.

47

Of men, women, and pie-slicing

What is the difference between men and women when they negotiate?"

You may consider this, as I do, a loaded question. So, let's look at a few research-based facts.

- When men and women negotiate against one another, such as in a buyer-seller arrangement, men get a larger slice of the pie, *but that does not have to be the case.*

- The key reason for the difference in how much men versus women are able to claim is traceable to their initial aspirations—their opening offers to be exact. Women, quite frankly, do not aspire to earn as much as men do, even when they are playing identical roles. Professor Linda Babcock noticed this and published a groundbreaking book called *Women Don't Ask*, which provides compelling evidence for the disparities we see at the negotiation table.

In my own research on this thorny subject with Laura Kray and Adam Galinsky, we wondered whether the typical stereotype of women being docile, nice, and nurturing might actually be hurting them. Indeed, we found that when women (and men) were reminded of the archetypal female stereotype of being accepting, nurturing, kind, and submissive, women claimed much less of the bargaining pie.

We obviously needed to try to turn around this situation. We found that two scenarios—mindsets—can really help women at the table. Let's call mindset number #1 the *backfire effect.* In one of our scientific tests, we decided to be up-front and center about the typical female stereotype. Rather than be politically correct and not say it or speak it, we clearly referenced the female stereotype as one in which females are accepting, giving, empathic, and so on. (We were banking on the fact that the high-powered females in our management and executive courses would think that this was a bunch of

> When men and women negotiate against one another, such as in a buyer-seller arrangement, men get a larger slice of the pie, but that does not have to be the case.

baloney.) They apparently did. They ended up claiming more of the pie than men did, and they claimed more of the pie than when we made absolutely no mention of the classic female stereotype. Thus, in some sense, if there is a gorilla in the room, it helps women to say that there is a gorilla in the room.

Several years ago, Professor Howard Raiffa compiled a list of 38 characteristics of successful negotiators in his book *The Art and Science of Negotiation*. As it turns out, some of those 38 characteristics are male-sounding (assertive, dominant), some are traditional female-sounding (empathic, good at nonverbal skills), and some have no gender connotations (punctual). When a mixed group of negotiators was given a redacted version of Professor Raiffa's list featuring the female-sounding "effective negotiator characteristics," the women in the group did much better than when they were given the male-redacted list or a neutral list. Everybody did the same negotiation. Despite the fact that everyone had the same objective financial situation and the same reservation price, the mindset we had created exerted a profound influence on how well the females in the group did. Let's call this the *right brain mindset*, which is the part of the brain that is skilled in language, nonverbal behavior, and so on.

> In some sense, if there is a gorilla in the room, it helps women to say that there is a gorilla in the room.

The point is not that men are taking advantage of women or treating them tougher than they would treat a male. But, rather, as Louis Pasteur once said, "Chance favors the prepared mind." Females who prepare their own mindsets should fare better in negotiation than those who don't.

48

Know why the fish swim

Cultural differences can dramatically affect negotiations. For example, when people from the U.S. and people from China were shown a picture of a group of swimming goldfish and asked to make a one-sentence summation of what was going on, the stories they told were diametrically different. Americans told stories of leadership and taking the helm. Stories about CEOs and their direct reports were not uncommon. People from China told stories about community members attempting to catch and protect a teammate and stories about how it is important to work in the community.

The U.S. stories were about leadership and individual effort. The Chinese stories were about community and team effort. These different stories illustrate one of the most profound differences among cultures: individualism versus collectivism.

Individualists see the world as their oyster. They see themselves as independent entities acting upon the world. They don't accept circumstances. They fight for what they want.

Collectivists see the world as a big tapestry, in which they represent one thread that makes a whole pattern. Collectivists take others into account when making decisions. They are willing to make adjustments so that the community can be best served.

Individualists and collectivists also give themselves away with their pronouns. Individualists use many more "I," "me," and "mine" pronouns; collectivists use many more "we,' "us," and "our" pronouns.

Cultural differences can also lead a negotiator into the barbed-wired fence of tradition.

One young woman from the U.S., Elisa, shared a depressing story about a cross-cultural negotiation in her company. She was 26 years of age and an engineer responsible for

> Individualists and collectivists also give themselves away with their pronouns. Individualists use many more "I," "me," and "mine" pronouns; collectivists use many more "we,' "us," and "our" pronouns.

product development. Her team, which happened to consist of three men, counted on her as their "knowledge leader."

Her trip to Asia was a complete failure, however. It was not because she failed to prepare. From the first moment of making contact with the counterparty, she was treated as a secretary. She was expected to take notes, make tea, and pick up supplies. The counterparty directed all conversation to the men on her team and did not acknowledge her. She was not invited to several key meetings—even though she was the lead negotiator.

My student had walked unsuspectingly into a hierarchical culture. *Hierarchical cultures* are traditional cultures that recognize males, tenure, seniority, and rank. Hierarchical cultures are based largely on who has status in society. Elisa lacked gray hair, and she had the wrong chromosomes. It did not matter that her team saw her as the lead negotiator; the counterparty did not acknowledge her. The senior people in hierarchical cultures are to be respected, and it is their job to take care of those who are dependent upon them.

Elisa, of course, had been a member of egalitarian status systems all her life. In egalitarian cultures, the merit of one's ideas determines one's status in an organization. In egalitarian status systems, there are status layers, but they are permeable through hard work and smarts.

According to negotiation expert Jeanne Brett, author of *Negotiating Globally*, the next time you negotiate with someone from a different culture, take the time to find out how that person views the world. Don't assume your view of the fish swimming is his story.

> The next time you negotiate with someone from a different culture, take the time to find out how that person views the world.

TRUTH

49

It does not make sense to always get to the point...

A recent study found that illustrated children's books in Asia and the U.S. have dramatically different kinds of facial expression on the characters. The facial expressions on the protagonists in U.S. children's books have wide, direct smiles and eyes that gaze at you. In contrast, the protagonists in Asian books have smiles that don't show a lot of teeth, and eye gaze is not penetratingly direct.

A common (but faulty) stereotype is that members of Asian cultures do not show emotions. However, the stereotype is false. The problem many people have is that we don't know how to read their emotions.

Some cultures, like in the U.S., are very direct in their emotional expression and communication. Other cultures, like in Japan, are more discreet.

> A common (but faulty) stereotype is that members of Asian cultures do not show emotions. However, the stereotype is false. The problem many people have is that we don't know how to read their emotions.

U.S. negotiators get down to business, say what they mean, present rational arguments, maintain eye contact, and challenge others outright. In contrast, members of indirect communication cultures (such as in Japan and Korea) put a greater value on helping others save face and thus, they will not directly challenge others when they disagree. This is why "yes" in some cultures does not mean agreement; it simply means, "I hear you." Moreover, members of indirect cultures may find it rude or inappropriate to ask direct questions about interests. Rather, people signal their interests indirectly, often by simply making offers.

The danger people make when they are tooling up to understand a person from a different culture is that they believe that there is little or no variation in the cultural group. This is why Professor Jeanne Brett, who wrote *Negotiating Globally*, distinguishes *cultural prototypes* from *cultural stereotypes*. Stereotypes are the simplistic belief that all members from a given culture behave and think the same way. In contrast, cultural prototypes recognize central tendencies as well as variation in cultures.

If you have gotten to the point of analyzing the counterparty on the three dimensions of culture, you are well on your way toward successful cross-cultural negotiation. The question will be, how much do you want to change? We need to wrestle with two considerations: (1) How much do I want to build and maintain a relationship with this other culture and (2) How much do I want to maintain my own cultural identity?[30] If I want to preserve my own culture but also bridge to another culture, then I need to integrate. If I care more about my own cultural values than yours, then I will separate. In some cases, I might be willing to put aside my own cultural values and embrace yours, which means I assimilate.

The danger people make when they are tooling up to understand a person from a different culture is that they believe that there is little or no variation in the cultural group.

TRUTH

50

Negotiating on the phone

Would you rather negotiate face to face or on the phone?

The face-to-face proponents say that you get more information from several data feeds when you are face to face. These students like the fact that they have access to a person's nonverbal as well as verbal behaviors.

Those who prefer the phone like the fact that they can use the phone as a buffer—to better compose their ideas and buy time.

Who is right? Actually, both are! If you are in a position of power, you are better off negotiating face to face because the other party is not able to counter-argue as effectively as you can. This can give you an edge when it comes to effective claiming. However, if you have less power relative to the other party, the phone provides a buffer by allowing you to better marshal your arguments and compose yourself.

When it comes to win-win agreements, there is a tendency for face-to-face negotiators to reach the most integrative outcomes, followed by telephone negotiators, and last, writing-only negotiators.[31]

Face-to-face interaction is the richest form of interaction because you have four channels of information feed:

- **Kinetic cues**—Kinetics means "touch," and in social interaction, touch is a way of establishing rapport. In negotiation, people establish rapport by shaking hands, high-fiving, pulling two chairs closer together, and so on.

- **Visual cues**—Visual cues include anything you can see about the other party, such as whether she maintains eye contact, how she uses her hands, whether her body language is dominating or submissive, emotional expressions on her face, and so on.

> If you are in a position of power, you are better off negotiating face to face because the other party is not able to counter-argue as effectively as you can.

- **Linguistic cues**—Linguistic cues refer to the actual content that negotiators use in their communication, such as the size of their offer.

- **Paralinguistic cues**—Paralinguistic cues refer to how a person uses language. For example, we can often detect sarcasm by the way a person emphasizes certain words.

When you negotiate on the phone, you lose the kinetic information feed and the visual information feed. This means you rely on linguistic cues and paralinguistic cues only. For this reason, people often have a harder time establishing rapport with the other person. Rapport is the feeling that you have when you are "in sync" or "on the same wavelength" with another person. Nonverbal behaviors, such as how you gesture and maintain eye contact and nod your head, are key to building rapport with someone. Have you ever had a phone call in which you and the other person were interrupting each other? This is a failure to synchronize.

When you communicate face to face with someone, you engage in a complex dance of sorts, in which you adjust your speech and bodies to ease social interaction. This social dance paves the way for more win-win agreements. In one investigation, some negotiators stood face to face, whereas others had to stand side by side (and

> Rapport is the feeling that you have when you are "in sync" or "on the same wavelength" with another person.

therefore, could not easily establish conversational rhythm based on bodily cues). The face-to-face negotiators reached deals more quickly and successfully averted a strike![32]

If you find yourself on the phone, rather than face to face, think about how to develop rapport with the counterparty. Here are some strategies that may pave the way toward smoother interaction:

- Engage in small talk or schmooze for the first five minutes, before getting down to action.

- Arrange for a short, face-to-face meeting before the phone call. (Having met someone face to face even one time can provide a foundation for rapport down the road.)

- Don't multitask when you are on the phone. (Shut off your email, and don't call this person when you are simultaneously checking into your hotel.) If you are dividing your attention, you are unable to focus on the interaction, and you send a signal to the other party that she is not worth your time.

- One of the most problematic things about phone calls is turn-taking. Signal that you are finishing speaking your turn by saying something like, "Well now that I have laid that out, I'm interested in your thoughts."

- End the phone call on the personal. People tend to remember beginnings and ends, so close on a bright note.

51

Your reputation

Think about your past 10 negotiations. How many were one-shot negotiations, in which you did not expect to see this person or his company ever again? How many were repeated-game negotiations, in which you would probably see this person or his company in the future?

Chances are, less than 10 percent of your negotiations are truly one shot. This being the case means that you need to think about and protect your reputation in most negotiations.

Think of your reputation as your social capital at the negotiation table. Your reputation is composed of three different things: (1) the personal brand or image you project; (2) people's firsthand dealing with you; and (3) secondhand information about you (gossip).

> Chances are, less than 10 percent of your negotiations are truly one shot. You need to think about and protect your reputation in most negotiations.

In one investigation of the reputations earned by students in a negotiation class,[33] the students rated one another on the basis of firsthand experience. Four different kinds of reputations surfaced:

- **Lair-manipulator**—This is someone who is willing to do anything to gain advantage.

- **Tough-but-honest**—This negotiator is known to be very tough, makes few concessions, but does not lie.

- **Nice and reasonable**—This negotiator is willing to make concessions.

- **Cream puff**—This negotiator will make concessions and be conciliatory regardless of what the other party does.

Before reading further, what would be the reputation you would want to have in your own negotiation community? As it turns out, people treat you differently, depending upon your reputation. If you have a reputation of being manipulative, people act more competitively with you.

How we see ourselves is not necessarily how others see us. Take the case of deceptive behavior: Most negotiators believe that they are deceived on average 40 percent of the time. (Sometimes the rate is about 50 percent.) However, these same people admit to using deception in about 25 percent of their negotiations. Do these two statistics add up?

Most negotiators believe that they are deceived on average 40 percent of the time. (Sometimes the rate is about 50 percent.) However, these same people admit to using deception in about 25 percent of their negotiations.

No, they don't add up. Why? I think there is one key reason: the double-standard effect. Quite simply, we evaluate others much more harshly than we look at ourselves. I am quick to believe that you misled me, but I rationalize my own behavior. It really does not matter how you look at yourself. You must consider your own reputation.

Be aware of the effects that result from the way you interact with the other parties during negotiation. The self-aggrandizing effect and gender effect may seem obvious ones to avoid. But recall that the *way* you make statements has effects as well. When you point to the disposition of the other party, such statements give rise to two biases about other people: the *halo effect* and the *forked-tail effect*. The halo effect is the tendency to believe that if a person is smart, she is also kind. The halo effect is the tendency to believe that if a person is physically attractive, she is also witty. In short, a halo effect occurs when people generalize wildly on the basis of only one piece of good information. You can probably guess what the forked-tail bias is: If you are clumsy, I also am inclined to think you are unintelligent, and so on.

The way you approach and respect others, then, has a great deal to do with how they do the same to you, and that, in a nutshell, is your reputation.

52

Building trust

Trust in a negotiation is like lubricant in a car engine: Things go a lot more smoothly. Three types of trust operate in our relationships:

- Deterrence-based trust
- Knowledge-based trust
- Identification-based trust

Deterrence-based trust is based on the principle of carrots and sticks. If I want you to perform work for me, I might give you an incentive to complete a contracting job by offering you a bonus for finishing before schedule. (I offer you a carrot.) I might also have a penalty clause. (If you fail to finish the job by a certain date, I reduce the payment.) Deterrence-based trusts are often based on contracts and monitoring. For example, if I hire you to work for me as a child-care provider, and I install a hidden video camera to monitor your behavior, this is a form of deterrence-based trust.

Deterrence-based trust is fairly expensive to use. (Think about the costs of the video camera and attorney's fees!) The other problem is that if you get wind that I am monitoring you, you might be upset. For example, the presence of signs reading, "Do not write on these walls under any circumstances" actually increases incidences of vandalism as compared to signs that say, "Please do not write on these walls" or having no sign at all![34]

For these reasons, many people in the business world use a different form of trust, known as knowledge-based trust. *Knowledge-based trust* is what is commonly referred to as a "gentleman's agreement" or "handshake understanding." Knowledge-based trust is trust that develops between people who have worked with each other long enough to feel that they know the other persona and understand them and can predict their behavior. To be sure, knowledge-based agreements are not binding in a court of law,

Knowledge-based agreements are not binding in a court of law, but they often have a binding effect on the people who make these agreements.

but they often have a binding effect on the people who make these agreements.

Most people prefer to work with people who are referred to them by a friend or colleague. Suppliers who regularly negotiate with certain customers are working on the basis of knowledge-based trust. Interestingly, the diamond market in New York is based on knowledge-based trust. Knowledge-based trust is based on the fact that you and I are in a community in which we both have reputations and we both want to maintain our reputation.

If knowledge-based trust is based upon my knowledge of you, identification based trust is based on the fact that we have aligned incentives. In *identification-based trust* systems, we have mutual empathy for each other. Identification-based trust means that other people have your value system—shared interests, values, and reactions to jointly experienced stimuli. For example, "You and I have the same high work ethic that comes from growing up where we did and putting ourselves through college." You should do your homework to find such commonalities and be sure to emphasize them. It is far easier to trust someone who you feel is on the same page as you in life.

Identification based trust is based on the fact that we have aligned incentives. In identification-based trust systems, we have mutual empathy for each other.

TRUTH

53

Repairing broken trust

Sometimes trust is broken in a relationship. How do you repair broken trust? Unfortunately, there is no surefire solution. Consider one of the following strategies.

Let them vent

People want to be heard. Letting people vent and blow off their steam does not mean you agree with them. It just means you are listening. So, let the person who feels wronged tell his side of the story. You don't have to agree; you just have to listen. Check to make sure you understand by summarizing what the other is saying. Ask the counterparty if you've got his side of the story straight.

> You don't have to agree; you just have to listen.

Apologize

If you did something you regret, say so. If you failed to do something you wished you'd done, say so. Make sure the other person hears your apology loud and clear. One of the best ways to apologize is to do something symbolic. Send a colleague a bouquet of flowers or a hand-written note (as opposed to dashing off an email) or give her a bottle of her favorite wine with a note saying, "I'm sorry about what happened."

The problem is, many people think they don't have anything to apologize for. In other words, they don't feel they did anything wrong. In that case, apologize that there was a misunderstanding. I like all of the following sentences.

> "I'm sorry that there has been so much confusion and anxiety around the issue of the new senior hire."
>
> "I'm sorry you did not get the email that was sent out."
>
> "I'm sorry that this situation has caused you so much stress."

Focus on the future

Saying you are sorry is often an uncomfortable act. Resist the urge to revisit the past in excruciating detail. Instead, focus on the future. What can you do to make sure that this misunderstanding does not happen again?

Do a relationship checkup

Don't wait for misunderstanding to occur before you talk about how things are going. Do a relationship checkup before problems occur. Pop your head into this person's office and simply ask, "How are things going concerning [the product development/the budget allocations/the hiring of new staff]? Is there anything that I should be working on to make sure that I am following through with our discussion about this? It is important to me that we work smoothly and I don't disappoint you."

Don't wait for misunderstanding to occur before you talk about how things are going.

Go overboard

Ironically, it is often when trust is breached that you get a once-in-a-lifetime opportunity to do something so wonderful for this person that he will never forget it. Let's say something happens that was not your fault but which shakes the trust of your professional relationship. Materials you sent arrived late and were ripped and smudged, unusable. You quickly send replacement materials, but don't stop there. You include a personalized gift for everyone involved. Sure, it can cost, but the other party's trust is often restored, and your obvious over-the-top effort to make things right might even lead to more business that would not have occurred otherwise.

References

Truth 1

1 Osborn, A. F. (1963). *Applied Imagination* (3rd ed.). New York, NY: Scribner.

Truth 4

2 Galinsky, A. D., and Mussweiler, T. (2001). "First offers as anchors: The role of perspective-taking and negotiator focus." *Journal of Personality and Social Psychology*, 81, 657-669.

Truth 6

3 Lax, D. A. and Sebenius, J. K., (1986). *The Manager as Negotiator*. New York, NY: Simon & Schuster, Inc. Labor economists Bill Walton and Bob McKersie refer to these two goals as the "mixed-motive" aspect of negotiation and warn that negotiators must balance creating value with claiming it. David Lax and Jim Sebenius argue that good negotiators do two things: they create value and they claim value. They are the "twin tasks of negotiation" and an effective manager-negotiator needs both skills.

Truth 7

4 Thompson, L. L., and Hastie, R. (1990). "Social perception in negotiation." *Organizational Behavior and Human Decision Processes*, 47, 98–123 and Thompson, L. L., and Hrebec, D. (1996). "Lose-lose agreements in interdependent decision making." *Psychological Bulletin*, 120, 396–409.

5 Tinsley, C. H., O'Connor, K. M., and Sullivan, B. A. (2002). "Tough guys finish last: The perils of a distributive reputation." *Organizational Behavior and Human Decision Processes*, 88, 621- 642.

Truth 9

6 Fisher, R. and William Ury, W. (1983). *Getting to Yes: Negotiating Agreement Without Giving In*, New York: Penguin Books.

Truth 14

7 Galinsky, A. D., and Mussweiler, T. (2001). "First offers as anchors: The role of perspective-taking and negotiator focus." *Journal of Personality and Social Psychology,* 81, 657-669.

Truth 20

8 Morris, M., Nadler, J., Kurtzberg, T., and Thompson, L. (2002). "Schmooze or lose: Social friction and lubrication in e-mail negotiations." *Group Dynamics,* 6, 89-100

Truth 22

9 Raiffa, H. (1982). *The Art and Science of Negotiation.* Belknap Press of Harvard University Press.

Truth 24

10 Kahneman, D., and Tversky, A. (1979). "Prospect theory: An analysis of decision under risk." *Econometrica,* 47, 263-291.

11 Fry, W. R., Firestone I., and Williams, D.L. (1983). "Negotiation process and outcome of stranger dyads and dating couples: Do lovers lose?" *Basic and Applied Psychology,* 4(1), 1-

12 In 1983, Max Bazerman and Margaret Neale coined the term "fixed-pie perception" to refer to this spurious belief. "Heuristics in Negotiation: Limitations to Effective Dispute Resolution." *Research in Organizational Behavior,* 9, 247-288.

13 I began to ponder how entrenched the fixed-pie perception was. For example, I wondered whether people in perfect agreement in reality would still see themselves in complete conflict. If one sister wanted oranges and the other wanted apples, would they still falsely assume that they were in competition? To investigate this, I created a scenario in which people negotiated face to face over eight issues. Two of the eight issues were ones in which negotiators had perfectly compatible interests, which should have resulted in full, mutually beneficial agreement on those issues. Depressingly, 25 percent of negotiators suboptimized on those issues, settling for something worse than what both of them wanted, a needless sacrifice. And among those who actually optimized on that issue, more than 50 percent did not know that

they had optimized (that the other party had interests perfectly compatible with theirs). This was major empirical evidence of the pervasiveness of win-lose thinking.

Truth 25

14 Lax, D. A. and Sebenius, J. K., (1986). *The Manager as Negotiator.* New York, NY: Simon & Schuster, Inc.

Truth 26

15 Pruitt, D.G. and Lewis, S.A. (1975). "Development of integrative solutions in bilateral negotiation." *Journal of Personality and Social Psychology*, 31, 621-630 and Carnevale, P.J., Pruitt, D.G., and Seilheimmer, S. (1981). "Looking and competing: Accountability and visual access in integrative bargaining." *Journal of Personality and Social Psychology*, 40, 111-120.

Truth 27

16 Frustrated by the low incidence of question asking and information sharing by negotiators, I took a drastic measure: I coached them to reveal information. In one investigation, I told negotiators in no uncertain terms to provide information to the other party. In the study, I compared three groups of people: revealers, questioners, and a control group. I told the revealers to share their interests with the other party, and the questioners to ask about the counterparty's interests. The control group received no specific instructions.

The results were dramatic: The revealers and the questioners did much better than the control group in terms of win-win deals. Thus, the revealers and the questioners advanced toward the Pareto Optimal Frontier, while the control group satisficed. So, whether you ask or provide information in a negotiation is less important than just getting it out in the open.

Moreover, the effects tended to multiply over time, meaning that as revealers and questioners completed more and more negotiations, they improved their outcomes at a faster rate than the control group. Keep in mind that nothing was preventing the control group from revealing their interests or asking questions. We just relied on their natural reluctance.

We did one more critical experiment before telling the world of negotiators that it's not only okay to reveal information, but that it's also one of the smartest things to do. Specifically, we had to show that revealing information wouldn't increase the risk of exploitation. So we set up a study in which one negotiator was told to reveal information to the opponent, but the opponent was to avoid revealing any information. This created an asymmetrical situation in which one party knew the interests of the other party, but not vice versa. Afterward, we looked for all possible evidence of exploitation, namely poorer performance by the lesser-informed negotiator. We found no evidence of exploitation. In fact, these asymmetrical-pairs were much better at expanding the pie and reaching win-win deals on average than the control groups.

Truth 36

17 Tajfel, H. (1970). "Experiments in intergroup discrimination." *Scientific American*, 223, 96-102.

18 Suedfeld, P., Bochner, S., and Matas, C. (1971). "Petitioners attire and petition signing by peace demonstrators: A field experiment." *Journal of Applied Social Psychology*, 1(3), 278-283.

Truth 37

19 Tversky, A. and Kahneman, D. (1974). "Judgment under uncertainty: Heuristics and biases." *Science*, 185, 1124-1131.

20 The 53 UN member States of the African Institute are the following: Algeria, Angola, Benin, Botswana, Burkina Faso, Burundi, Cameroon, Cape Verde, Central African Republic, Chad, Comoros, Congo, Côte d'Ivoire, Democratic Republic of Congo, Djibouti, Egypt, Equatorial Guinea, Eritrea, Ethiopia, Gabon, Gambia, Ghana, Guinea Bissau, Guinea, Kenya, Lesotho, Liberia, Libyan Arab Jamahiriya, Madagascar, Malawi, Mali, Mauritania, Mauritius, Morocco, Mozambique, Namibia, Niger, Nigeria, Rwanda, Sao Tome e Principe, Senegal, Seychelles, Sierra Leone, Somalia, South Africa, Sudan, Swaziland, Tanzania, Togo, Tunisia, Uganda, and Zimbabwe.

Truth 38

21 Tversky, A. and D. Kahneman. (1981). "The framing of decisions and the psychology of choice." *Science*, 211, 45-58.

22 Bazerman, M. H. Magliozzi, T., and Neale, M. A. (1985). "Integrative bargaining in a competitive market." *Organizational Behavior and Human Decision Processes*, 35(3), 294–313.

Truth 39

23 The study was made by my colleagues Ashleigh Rosette of Duke University and Shirley Kopelman of University of Michigan. Kopelman, S., Rosette, A.S., Thompson, L. (2006) "The Three Faces of Eve: Strategic Displays of Positive, Negative, and Neutral Emotions in Negotiations." *Organizational Behavior and Human Decision Processes* 99, 81-101.

24 O'Quin K, Aronoff J. 1981. "Humor as a technique of social influence." *Social Psychology Quarterly*, 44, 349-357.

Truth 40

25 Ury, W., Brett, J.M., Goldberg, S.B. (1993). *Getting Disputes Resolved*. San Francisco, CA: Jossey-Bass.

Truth 42

26 White, J. B., Tynan, R., Galinsky, A. D., and Thompson, L. (2004). "Face threat sensitivity in negotiation: Roadblock to agreement and joint gain." *Organizational Behavior and Human Decision Processes, 94*, 102-124.

Truth 44

27 Drigotas, S. M., Whitney, G. A., and Rusbult, C. E. (1995). "On the peculiarities of loyalty: A diary study of responses to dissatisfaction in everyday life." *Personality and Social Psychology Bulletin*, 21, 596–609.

Truth 45

28 Brett, J. M. (2001). *Negotiating Globally: How to Negotiate Deals, Resolve Disputes, and Make Decisions Across Cultural Boundaries.* San Francisco, CA: Jossey-Bass.

29 Brett, J.M. (2007). "Negotiation Strategies for Managers." Executive Program, Kellogg School of Management.

Truth 49

30 In my research with Susan Brodt and Erica Peterson, we compared three types of negotiations: one on one; team on team; and a team negotiating against a solo negotiator. The incidence and volume of win-win agreements were dramatically greater when there was a team at the bargaining table. Moreover, it was not necessary that both parties be represented by teams. As long as one of the parties at the table was a team, this moved everyone toward the Pareto Optimal Frontier.

Truth 50

31 Valley, K.L., Moag, J., and Bazerman, M.H. (1998). A matter of trust: Effects of communication on the efficiency and distribution of outcomes. *Journal of Economic Behavior and Organizations*, 34, 211-238.

32 Drolet, A.L., and Morris, M.W. (2000). "Rapport in conflict resolution: Accounting for how non-verbal exchange fosters cooperation on mutually beneficial settlements to mixed-motive conflicts." *Journal of Experimental Social Psychology*, 36, 26-50.

Truth 51

33 Croson, R. and Steven G. (2001). "Reputations in negotiation." In Hoch, S.J., Kunreuther, H.C., and Gunther, R.E. (Eds.), *Wharton on making decisions (pp.177-186). Hoboken, NJ: John Wiley and Sons.*

Truth 52

34 Pennebaker, J.W., and Sanders, D.Y. (1976). "American graffiti: Effects of authority and reactance arousal." *Personality and Social Psychology Bulletin*, 2, 264-267.

Acknowledgments

In negotiation, there is always a "hidden table," or a group of people who are the real decision makers that might not be visible. This book is no exception. This book is lovingly dedicated to all the students who've suffered through my MBA and executive classes throughout the 20 years that I've been teaching. Their questions, provocations, and stories are echoed in this book. Silva Kurtisa and Melissa Martin at the Kellogg Teams and Groups Center pulled together the drafts and made order out of chaos. Russ Hall and Sachin Waikar did fantastic editing of my feeble drafts. My colleagues and collaborators, Max Bazerman, Jeanne Brett, Adam Galinsky, Shirli Kopelman, Laura Kray, Jeff Loewenstein, Kathleen McGinn, Don Moore, Michael Morris, Janice Nadler, Ashleigh Rosette, Elizabeth Seeley, and Judith White provided the intellect and enthusiasm to build a community of negotiation research that inspired this book. My family, Anna, Ray, Sam, and Bob, gave me the encouragement to keep on plugging when I did not feel like plugging any more.

About the Author

Leigh Thompson is a Distinguished Professor of Dispute Resolution & Organizations at the Kellogg School of Management at Northwestern University. She directs the Leading High Impact Teams executive program, the Kellogg Team and Group Research Center, and co-directs the Negotiation Strategies for Managers program. An active scholar and researcher, she has published more than 95 research articles and chapters and has authored 7 books, including: *The Mind and Heart of the Negotiator (3rd Edition)*, *Making the Team (3rd edition)*, and *Organizational Behavior Today (in press)*; and edited 5 books, including: *Creativity and Innovation in Organizational Teams, Shared Knowledge in Organizations, Negotiation: Theory and Research, The Social Psychology of Organizational Behavior,* and *Conflict in Organizational Groups (in press)*.

Thompson speaks and conducts workshops on negotiation skills across the globe. Some of her clients include: Bristol-Meyers Squibb, Microsoft, Chubb Insurance, Corn Products International, Sears Holdings, Baxter Healthcare, Chiquita Brands, Lamb Weston, CDW, Fleet Financial, Heller Financial, Novartis, as well as Sandia National Laboratories and the Central Intelligence Agency.

Visit her at: www.LeighThompson.com.

Simply the best thinking

The **Truth About** Series offers the collected and distilled knowledge on a topic and shows you how you to apply this knowledge in your everyday life.

Creating a team of self-motivated individuals who love their jobs is possible. Learn how, regardless of budget or industry.

ISBN: 0132381869
Martha Finney
$18.99

Great people don't want to work for desperate employers. It's a war for talent, and you need to win.

ISBN: 0132381869
Cathy Fyock
$18.99

Learn real solutions for problems faced by every manager in this definitive, evidence-based guide to effective management.

ISBN: 0132346036
Stephen P. Robbins
$18.99

Coming in Spring 2008

The Truth About Presenting
The Truth About Decision Making
The Truth About Change
The Truth About Avoiding Scams